NOBLE SOUL

NOBLE SOUL

The Mystical Sciences of The Man,

The Moor and The Message

**BROTHER
ERIC MUNGIN BEY D.M.**

Copyright © 2015 Eric Mungin Bey D.M.

Published by WordVision

All rights reserved. No part of this publication may be reproduced, stored in a retrieval system or transmitted, in any form, or by any means, electronic, mechanical, recorded, photocopied, or otherwise, without the prior written permission of both the copyright owner and the above publisher of this book, except by a reviewer who may quote brief passages in a review.

The scanning, uploading, and distribution of this book via the Internet or via any other means without the permission of the publisher is illegal and punishable by law. Please purchase only authorized electronic editions and do not participate in or encourage electronic piracy of copyrightable materials. Your support of the author's rights is appreciated.

Designed by Vince Pannullo
Printed in the United States of America by RJ Communications.

ISBN:917-0-9966982-07

Contents

An Introduction and Overview 7

Chapter I: The Man 11
Chapter II: The Moor 41
Chapter III: The Message 75
Origin of El and Bey 106
Know Thyself 114
Gratitude Bro. Hommett A El 118
Reincarnation Bro. John Givens El 122

Dedication 137
This Book 139
References 141

An Introduction and Overview

YOU are about to enter into the words of science, every word, letter and numbers are symbols that has its hidden meaning. I only ask of you to read this information with a non judgmental mind. The reason why is because the human mind has been programmed from the various stages of development. For example, from the time at the age of one years old to seven., a child's brain is like a empty computer. The brain was constructed to operate by its maker or if you will by its master, this maker or master controls their environment in which we live in and what ever a child see and hear they will absorb what is given to them. Some of us would not admit that their minds has not been programmed or think that they have been manipulated by the maker or master who governs our world. But why?

Because who ever control your mind knows that you will make a better slave. Now a child's mind is like a empty disk which has been programmed with truth and falsehood, however the child must learn the difference between what is right and what is wrong. The outcome of the programmed mind affects their thinking, reasoning and understanding. By this time their minds conceive a certain perception about life accepting whatever operating system that has been install in their brain. I want you to take this time to search within the mind how people get misled and believe some- thing that might not be true. A huge deception has been played on our minds that has affected our lives. We believe in what man thinks perhaps is truth instead of knowing the absolute truth.

My main purpose for sharing this information is, because my mind was programmed when I was a child. But there was something in me as I know there is something in you who truly wants to know the absolute truth. Because by knowing the truth it will set you free, practicing the truth and you will stay free. At times it may be difficult to understand and explain why? Because of our thoughts, we think at times in a normal mental processes and other times those processes become hi- jacked and exaggerated. So the result that we are thinking of what you feel is unable to find the dividing line between the reality of the true self or the illusion of falsehood that controls our world today. At times our brain can be motivated by a drive of negative emotions and because the lack of knowledge of self we do not know how to redirect this negative emotion into a positive connection that will lead us to the awakening of the truth.

Our thinking must evolve not bound by evidence of the senses and not allow the processes of our mind and brain under the maker or master of their belief. A controlled thinker in their belief in the paranormal reflects normal brain activity carried to an extreme. By this activity of the mind we cannot think beyond the reach of reasoning. Therefore, we will no longer think logic. Remember this, a great de- ception can only take place where there is lack of knowledge. You see, we as human beings have a divided mind. This was programmed into our minds to cause a conflict between religion, race, rich and the poor. It is the science of cause and affect, to understand more of our mind one must know the cause which is your false thinking. The affect, is to keep everyone distracted with a multitude of issues. The maker or master knows that if they cannot program a child from the age of one to seven years old. They will attempt to try from fourteen to twenty-one by this time the young brain can be infected with a virus such as negative energy put out through wave links in our music, programmed television, radio, food, drugs, news papers, magazines. Without realizing it, our minds has been conquered. Unknowingly you will be told what too listen, what to wear, what to eat, what to buy, what to read and what to say. I know we make our choice to what we want, but that is it. We should make our choice in life of what we need and not by what we want. Without realizing, some of our so-called Black people or African American minds has been manipulated in a cunning and devious ways through religion, music, his-story, laws, and broken treaties. Often at times we allow our emotions to override our logic thinking. Therefore , we are subject to accept our emotional idea of what we think as Truth. Some will defend it without any questions. There is no reasoning, nor an attempt to analysis it. No evaluation towards the subject in matter. Over whelm by our emotional perception we have replaced the Absolute Truth with false thinking and finally we become false within ourselves. **Noble Drew Ali 's** divine instructions was a prescription for deprogramming the human mind. These lesson's were put in place to override the existing information that was placed in our minds. This was necessary to deprogram the human mind. How did the Prophet begin to uplift the Moorish Americans?

The key to the answer is in the question (begin) by teaching them to be themselves. The science to begin. Meaning **Noble Drew Ali** started to do something that was not being done before and bring into being. He caused something to come into existence. By us not knowing ourselves, we rely on what was told to us of who we are. Therefore, our minds has been enslaved on what we become of what we do not know. And with our pretended thinking we appear as though we do not want to be taught not just by anyone. **Noble Drew Ali** said "he is here to teach us about ourselves," Now his words are the past, the future and the present. If we are willing to be taught we must become a student, and our teacher will appear. And he is in the likeness of **Noble Drew Ali**. Teaching them to be themselves in other words think for yourself. Have an independent mind. More than we ever know, **Noble Drew Ali** handed us something he said we cannot tear up.

His words are a hidden treasure for the human soul either you learn to reach that state or as he said return to the state were I the prophet found you. **Noble Drew Ali** was divinely prepared in such away that we will have to go back to the state of mind of our forefather's to understand his spiritual will. By 1925 at the age of 39 **Prophet Noble Drew Ali** has reach the third level of self consciousness. This higher form of consciousness is a matter of the maturity of the soul. This completement of cycle of souls pilgrimage and service. Therefore not subject to what we know as time. Please do not be confused with **Noble Drew Ali's** physical presence, but realize his spiritual presence is timeless. It has always been and it will always be. This wonderful degree of spiritual consciousness, that **Noble Drew Ali** has become this silent power. His personal presence of pure energy shows within his eyes demonstrate the State of spiritual liberation.

Peace and Love, Conscious Communicator

CHAPTER I

THE MAN

NOBLE **Drew Ali** said: **"That every word I speak is spirit, and you Moors better heed."** Man is not the body, nor the soul; he is a spirit and a part of our father ALLAH. Behind every name there is a sacred power. The name Timothy which means "Honoring the Universal Creator" The essence of his spiritual seed that was planted here on earth in which he holds deep within himself the attributes of our creator. The I is the primary vowel[1], it represent the element of fire. Fire is a powerful vibration. During his youthful age Timothy had a drive to find something that is fulfilling in life. No matter what circumstances he always remain humble. The I, also holds a science of a tremendous healing ability. This was useful on May the 16th, 1927 (see flyer on page 13.) Drew which means to move with force[2]. By honoring ALLAH, He was obeying his will. The science behind his name Timothy Drew was the preparation for Prophet Noble Drew Ali.[3] He was a noble[4] brother from the Cherokee nation. The spirit which means real essence of energy that dwells within us. This is the

---

[1] In ancient sciences, all vowels were the key to our health and soul. HK of the MHTS Chap. 38 The Soul Of Man V1 What health is to the body even that is honesty to the soul. Timothy is a highly capable individual, a man whose scope of vision can extend far beyond his own boundaries. His name will allow him to use his intelligence in the area of the hard sciences.

[2] HK of the M. H. T. of S 1927 Chap. 7 Jesus Explains To Lamaas The Meaning Of Truth V16 Force is the will of ALLAH and is omnipotent. Drew is first and foremost a thinker who loves to play with conceptsand possibilities.

[3] Ibid. Chap. 48 The End of Time And The Fulfiling Of The Prophesies V1 Noble Drew Ali was divinely prepared in due time by ALLAH.

[4] Noble which means high moral character,. as honor, generosity, or courage (a noble soul) Super in nature:Exalted.

very key to our existence beyond our physical appearances. However, that is all forgotten we depend upon our carnal self, the body of desires. Shallow men judge merit by noise and this is what the thoughtless think. We should judge men by what they are and not what they seem to be. Noble Drew Ali truly was the man weather you accept him or not. His words was right on time when the truth was needed. His works are not forgotten for those who understand his mission for the lost souls of humanity and let us not forget his benevolent deeds that continue from generation to generation. You may ask what was his motivation? Love my friend it was love coming from the utmost part of his existence. Born January 8th 1886[5] the end of time and the fulfilling of the prophesies[6].

---

[5] The true sign of a Prophet in America was written in code. 1886 was the footnote from the Holy Quran by Maulana Muhammad Ali , seventh edition (1985) which also is coded 8+5=13 the year that Noble Drew Ali begin his mission was 1913. Chapter (28) - 1928 Is when he held his first Moorish convention. The Narrative Section 6: The Truth of Revelation The broad points of likeness in the principles of two different prophets appearing at such a distance of time from each other, among entirely different nations, and under totally different circumstances, and the fulfillment of the prophecies uttered by one in the other.

[6] HK of the M. H. T. of S 1927 Chap. 48 The End Of Time And The Fulfilling of The Prophesies.

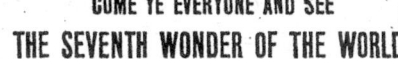

Honorable mention from the statements of Prophet Noble Drew Ali. From Brother B. Cook Bey The Holy Prophet had healing nights at the Temple where he healed people. He healed people in Baltimore Maryland as well as Chicago.

The science of his birth shown to us through numerology. His Birth path number is 5. The Birth path or Life path shows what you are here to do. The 5 is known as the master sage. It said that change will be a recurring event throughout your life, and you will welcome these changes as gateways to new opportunities and the develop- ment of free will. With time you will become a defender of freedom. You will view the world through liberal's eyes, and will most likely champion the causes of the world's underdogs. Now can you really see his true path! Noble Drew Ali began in Newark N. J. as the Canaanite Temple in the year of 1913. By 1916 It was known as Moorish Divine and National Movement, by moving to Chicago he organized the Moorish Holy Temple of Science in the year 1925. On November 29th 1926 it was The Moorish Temple of Science and it was later change to The Moorish Science Temple of America, May 2,1928. Out of all these changes what remains is Noble Drew Ali's principles Love, Truth, Peace Freedom and Justice. That is the true foundation of his lessons. His Soul number is 9, let us read carefully what this means. This number describes your deepest desires and dreams and the person you truly want to be. You are the essence of compassion and love[7] for your fellow man as well as the universe[8]. You desire to create[9] harmony[10], peace and beauty for all of us. Your compassion will often lead you to sacrifice[11] your own needs to address those of others. Now this lead us to his personality number, this reveals the "external you" the personality traits others will know you. My former teacher Brother Hommett A. El was a student under Noble Drew Ali, he was inducted into the adept chamber in the year of 1928 by Noble Drew Ali, he said that Noble Drew Ali was the most

---

[7] Noble Drew Ali said repeatedly that "We need to learn to Love instead of hate."

[8] HK of the M. H. T. of S 1927 Chap. 46-V9 All nations of the earth in these modern days are seeking peace, but there is but one true and divine way that peace may be obtained in these days and it is through Love, Truth, Peace, Freedom and Justice being taught universally to all nations, in all lands.

[9] Ibid. chap. 12-V9 ALLAH never made a heaven for man; He never made a Hell; we are creators and make our own.

[10] Ibid. Chap. 3-V11 The higher self is mother of the virtues and the harmonies of life.

[11] Ibid. Chap. 8-V22 Make human hearts your altars, and burn your sacrifices with the fire of love.

humble person that he has ever met. The personality number of Noble Drew Ali is 7. The sign of 7 shows us that this person is deeply absorbed in the pursuit of spiritual[12] and cosmic knowledge. 7s are intelligent, perceptive and introspective. They have the air of a mystic about them and can be quite aloof. Also 7s love their privacy.[13] How ever, the 7 Personalities wisdom and knowledge will draw people to them, and in the end they will realize sharing their knowledge is as rewarding as gaining it. And now the 3 is his maturity number. This reveals the person you will come to be your true self[14]. In his early years he had spent much time bringing his creative talents and ability to bring the best out in others[15] to the forefront. We go through many human stages of life, Age 7 is the age of reason; twice that, fourteen, is puberty; thrice that, twenty-one, is the age of maturity. That will brings us to this Pinnacle[16] which represent moments in your life in

---

[12] Noble Drew Ali was called to go to Egypt- After reaching the age of manhood, he went to Egypt, the Egyptian Sages who were the wise men of the East, knew of the coming of the Western Prophet before he set foot on Egyptian soil. When he arrived, the Sages took him to the Egyptian School were Jesus, Moses and many other Prophets attended before him. It is here that he went through the halls of learning. This school was known as "The School of the Prophets" Noble Drew Ali went 500 feet down into the secret Chambers where he conquered the spirits of Fire, Water, Earth and Air. The Sages put stripes on his back to prove to the outside world that he went into the secret chambers. Later Noble Drew Ali return back to America to start his great mission with the consciousness of the Moorish Holy Koran. He was first called, Professor Drew the Egyptian Adept.

[13] This is why Noble Drew Ali never revealed about his parents name and I must address here that he was so much a mystery that his birth certificate was not known . The State of North Carolina office of Vital Statistics law requiring the filling of Births and deaths with Vital Records did not become effective until October 1, 1913. The number 13 is the scared symbol of Afru-ika and the ancient Mexican people. He who understands the number 13 will be given a symbol of power and dominion (New ark) the ark represents a positive, saving state of consciousness, which agrees with or forms a covenant with the principle of Being.

[14] HK of the M. H. T. of S 1927 Chap. 3-V6 "The higher self is human spirit clothed with soul, made in the form of ALLAH."

[15] Moorish Literature are Excerpts taken from the Moorish Guide 1927-1928 Moorish Leader's Historical Message to America, Noble Drew Ali said: "Look for the best in others and give them the best that is in you."

[16] HK of the M. H. T. of S. 1927 Chap. 39 Pinnacle of Wisdom

which you realize current goals and learn some of life's lessons. Your First Pinnacle begins at birth and last until around the age of 27.[17] His Pinnacle number is 9 in this period where your love for your fellow man will be at its zenith. You will also play healer and inspirer to those around you. A 9 pinnacle is never easy, you will be asked to sacrifice meeting your own needs for the good of others. You may experience the pain[18] of loss, but in the end will be rewarded by fulfilling your soul needs, to ease the pain of others. The pains that we felt are the effects after slavery which brings us to the 5 categories of slavery. National, Mental, Socially, Economically and Moral. For those who live by his principles and the love of our Father-ALLAH. His teachings will not be in vain for that cause, for he is rewarded by his fulfillment. What is interesting here is that his Birth number is 8 this does have an effect on his life's path and destiny. It is said that this 8 have a very strong character and skills to be a successful leader. You should rise to the forefront. The 8 is also his personal year number, this tells you what is happening in your life this year. This is a year in which you should assert your leadership[19] as well as deal with any issues you have developed with authority.[20] The time for you to become empowered and realize your success comes from love. The divine essence in his name is the science of energy projecting the real man within the form. When he elevated his spirit through love he became a prophet, in his questionary, question 6 What is a prophet? A prophet is a thought[21] of ALLAH manifested in flesh. Not all forms are physical. A thought, for example is a form. (A thought is

---

[17] Prophet Noble Drew Ali begin his mission at the age of 27.

[18] Moorish Literature are Excerpts taken from the Moorish Guide 1927-1928 Prophet Makes Plea To Nation, Noble Drew Ali said: "I have suffered much and severely in the past through misunderstanding of what the movement was dedicated to."

[19] Ibid. Moorish Leader's Historical Message To America I am your affectionate leader. I shall continue to labor day and night, both in public and private, for your good, thereby contributing to the welfare of our country and its people as a whole.

[20] Ibid. Prophet Announces His Authority And Power

[21] HK of the M. H. T. of S 1927 Chap. 1 All thoughts of ALLAH are infinite. The thoughts of ALLAH, are everlasting of the past unto the never ending days to come. And so is man the spirit-man. Holy Bible King James version I Timothy 3:16 He who was manifest in flesh, justified in the Spirit.

energy) or light. And so this energy was formed within the flesh. Now so many people may say; a Prophet! Yes It is according to your understanding. A prophet means one who delivers divines messages or interprets the divine will. A religious leader, who foretells the future. The Prophet told the members in Chicago in a statement.

> "If a star and a crescent did not appear on December 18th then I am not a Prophet of ALLAH."

It was on a Friday, December 18, 1925, the star and the crescent appeared in the heavens, Our Universal Creator's sign to the people that Noble Drew Ali was to be the American Prophet. Who was to bring the true and divine creed of Islam to the people of America. On Saturday December 19, 1925 Chicago Daily Tribune published this rare science of the planet Venus and the Moon in conjunction. As always through our past time some people did not believe in our prophet's. It has been revealed in our Holy Books that to every nation there is a messenger.[22] It is also written that "We sent messengers, We have mentioned to thee before and messengers, We have not mentioned to thee[23]". In the book of Deuteronomy[24]

> "The Lord thy God will raise up unto thee a Prophet from the midst of thee; unto him ye shall hearken;" Saint John[25] "He came unto his own and his own received him not."

If you are still looking for answers or proof that Noble Drew Ali was a Prophet, then you must go to the source of truth. All truth comes from our Universal Creator Allah. And truth is but one; your doubts are from

---

[22] Holy Quran by Maulana Muhammad Ali 1917- Seventh edition 1985 Chapter 10 section 5-V47
[23] Ibid. 1917- Seventh edition 1985 Chapter 4 section 23- V64
[24] Holy Bible King James version Chap. 18-V15
[25] Ibid. Chap. 1-V11

your own thoughts.[26] Naturally do man desire the truth; yet, when it is before him, he will not apprehend it. The fault is not in truth, for that is amiable; but the weakness of man bareth not his splendor.[27]

CHICAGO DAILY TRIBUNE: SATURDAY, DECEMBER 19, 1925.

Crescent and Star

The symbol of Islam hung low in the western sky last night at sunset. The moon and the planet Venus were in conjunction, with Venus following the horns of the crescent. The figure of the crescent and star is one of the most beautiful sights of the heavens and is rather rare. It was much admired ages before Mohammed adopted it as his symbol. This conjunction was a bright one, as Venus is now nearing the earth. From the astronomer's viewpoint the event furnished an excellent chance to compare the brilliancy of the earth's two nearest celestial neighbors. The moon is our satellite, while Venus is the earth's twin world. The moon is a dead and frozen little globe, while Venus pulses with life like the earth.

---

[26] HK of the M. H. T. of S 1927 Chap. 42-V23

[27] Ibid. chap. 43-V20

1925 was the year when Noble Drew Ali announce his Prophet-hood, within the science and symbols of numbers 25/ 2+5= 7 this represent his spiritual guidance of our Moorish Nation circle 7. Friday is the 7th and Holy day.

We were mis- educated[28] by a system that enslaved our minds by training our mind on what to think. Noble Drew Ali said:

" If I can get you to think you can free your self "

Remember he taught us how to think and not what to think. We have remained, in the falsehood of darkness for so long, and when finally the knowledge of truth arrive, that brings us this consciousness[29] of light. Some of us became blinded from the radiance of the sun which brings us this energy of truth. Then we begin to shout! Turn that light out! Therefore rejecting the truth without opening our minds to the possibility that it may bring us to our real freedom. Free from being ignorance which mean to ignore the knowledge of self. Have you ever heard of the saying "What you don't know won't hurt you." Think about it, What you don't know will! Noble Drew Ali said:

"Rare is it that you find a real prophet whose mission is salvation of the nations. The land is full of false prophets whose mission is to fleece the people."[30]

---

[28] The MIS-EDUCATION of the Negro by Carter G. Woodson 1933 " when you control a man's thinking you do not have to worry about his actions."

[29] The conscious mind - it's our true education which means to "know thy self" your conscious mind is how you think. (This is your rational, logical mind.) It creates and develops your thoughts. Your thoughts has two aspects: the idea- the statement of thought, and the feelings associated with that thought. It proceeds to conclusion based on observation, experience and education. This first level of the conscious mind represents the world of effect. We are creators and make our own through our thoughts, so if there is a cause there is also an effect.

[30] Moorish Literature are Excerpts taken from the Moorish Guide 1927-1928 Savior of Humanity

His mission was to teach our people the truth about themselves and that they need to learn to love instead of hate, and to redeem the people from their sinful ways. For those who knew him, all have the same response. He was a humble brother, there are only good things to say about this man known as Prophet Noble Drew Ali and if any one think otherwise, then they must have been in their lower self.[31] Its like when you were in your teens and you have done something wrong and because of the love that your parents have for you, they punish you. So that you may know not to make that mistake again. So we get puffed up with anger, because we were told about your negative self. We as people do not like to be told about ourselves when we are doing wrong. Then we begin to slander those who tried to help us. This even goes for those who boast of their superior understanding with the semblance of truth, who are known as the pretended wise. For they are the very one's who fleece the people. Prophet Noble Drew Ali had congratulated the true Moors for their past loyalty and fidelity, because of certain incidents that came about in some of the temples, which seem to come from the fact that there are those who do not know where the seat of power is vested.[32] You see Noble Drew Ali was a very compassionate person when it came down to honor and respect as it was for our ancestors. Noble Drew Ali had study some exclusive mystic Sufism and oriental lessons from an early age. Therefore, he taught us to honor all divine prophets like Jesus, Mohammed, Buddha and Confucius. They all brought the same remedy for their nations. Thus Noble Drew Ali was a universal Prophet. He said:

"All nations of the earth in these modern days are seeking peace, but there is but one true and divine way that peace may be obtained

---

[31] HK of the M. H. T. of S 1927 Chap. 3-V11 The lower self breeds hatred, slander, lewdness, murder, theft and everything that harms.

[32] Moorish Literature are Excerpts taken from the Moorish Guide 1927-1928 Prophet Announces His Authority And Power

in these days and it is through Love, truth, Peace, Freedom and Justice being taught universally to all nations, in all lands."[33]

In the late 20's Brother T. Booker Bey said he saw 20 Arabians, 2 Chinese, and 1 Japananise join the Moorish Science Temple of America. Various Moors of the Prophet's time, said that when the prophet was at the Temple, you had to come early to get a seat, and they could not get in the front rows, because the Arabians, Indians, and other foreign Moslems were in those rows to hear and see Prophet Noble Drew Ali.[34] During the prophet's travels he met a man know as Abdul Aziz Ibn Suad[35] from Arabia, he believe in the Prophet so much he called him Sharif[36] Abdul Ali, because he was a servant[37] of ALLAH and by being a humble brother he has earned the title of Ali. Prophet Noble Drew Ali was an angel[38] to those who felt within his spiritual energy. All Divine Prophet's were an Angel manifested in human flesh. Their sole purpose is to act as spiritual mediators in their respectful sphere. The sacred name Angel means, The messenger of truth. Prophet Noble Drew Ali was an Angel of the third sphere, These Angels who function as heavenly messengers. They are to serve humanity.[39] The word Angel derives from Angiras (Sanskrit) which means a divine spirit. Person of exceptional holiness. Spiritual being attendant upon ALLAH. All Divine Prophet's has the same spirit, but they came in different times and forms. They are to deliver messages to the world. And from their

---

[33] HK of the M. H. T. of S 1927 Chap. 46-V9

[34] Statements and prophesies of the Prophet Noble Drew Ali

[35] Ibn Saud (1879-1953) He was the founder of the kingdom of Saudi Arabia by 1922 he takes the title of Sultan of Najd and its dependencies. 1924 Ibn Saud conquers Mecca . 1925 Madina surrenders to Ibn Saud. 1926 Declares himself as King of Hijaz, in addition to his Sultan position in Najd. 1932 Saudi Arabia is formed.

[36] Sharif (Noble) Abdul (Servant) Ali (Most High)

[37] HK of the M. H. T. of S 1927 p. 3 Noble Drew Ali said: "I am a prophet and servant is worthy of his hire.

[38] From the Moorish Koran Questionary Q 40. What is our Prophet to us? He is an Angel of ALLAH, who is sent to bring us the Everlasting Gospel of ALLAH.

[39] From the Moorish Koran Questionary Q15. For what purpose was the Moorish Holy Temple of Science founded? For the uplifting of fallen humanity .

messages we have our scared books.[40] He was born of the tenth sign of Capricorn[41]. They are the most persecuted and misunderstood of all signs. The parent of all mankind, chosen to govern and control, he must be faced all his life with difficult obstacles[42] that are not usual, so that he can be tried and tested, and found worthy[43] of the positions that will be entrusted to him, no other sign has such depth,[44] profoundly and sincerity.[45] He is trust worthier than many others and works patiently, with great perseverance. This is the key to his success. He is generous, yet practical, critical, yet forgiving. He is often misunderstood,[46] because he feels concern for all and does not hesitate to correct and chastise; just as a concerned parent would. This cardinal earth element sign is ruled by Saturn. Boundaries and self-discipline, as well as wisdom and stabilities are its domain. They love to undertake hardships to prove their caliber of facing and over coming any problems. They are always keen to seek answers to problems.[47] They wont stop until they get answers. Capricorn for being a teacher of valuable

---

[40] HK of the M. H. T. of S 1927 Chap. 2-V26 And when the world is ready to receive, lo ALLAH will send a messages to open the book and from its pages all the messages of purity and love.

[41] Capricorn is ruled by the planet Saturn. Which the planet gives telepathic energy to the subconscious.

[42] Moorish Literature is Excerpts taken from the Moorish Guide 1927-1928 Moorish Leader's Historical Message To America: "The Moorish Holy Temple of Science has received some opposition and criticism."

[43] HK of the M. H. T. of S 1927 p. 3 "As I am a prophet and the servant is worthy of his hire."

[44] Ibid. chap. 13-V16 "The highest heights are gained by those who reach the greatest depths; and you shall reach the greatest depths."

[45] Ibid. chap. 34-V2 "The tongue of the sincere is rooted in heart"

[46] Moorish Literature are Excerpts taken from the Moorish Guide 1927-1928 Prophet Makes Plea To Nation, Noble Drew Ali said: "I have suffered much and severely in the past through misunderstanding of what the movement was dedicated to."

[47] Ibid. The Voice of The Prophet " The Negro problem is being solved only as it can, and that is by the Moorish National Divine Movement."

lessons[48] which enable him to achieve and progress.[49] This ability is acquired piece by piece, they are patient. Capricorn is ruled by Saturn which makes this sign something of the wise man of the zodiac. He is careful, prudent, calculating and persevering. Saturn and Capricorn also provide the structure, stamina and endurance that enable him to pursue a dream to its manifest, his ability to commit and achieve is rooted in his capacity to take life and his aspirations seriously. All planets keep moving after you were born. At one point, they all come back to the position where they were when you were born. This is called a planetary return. Saturn takes about 29[50] years. This is called Saturn's return, the Saturn return represents a renewal of Saturn's energy in our lives, responsibility, authority, goals and restructuring. This goal[51] of Saturn's develop mental process to build an independent sense of self,[52] to establish one's own authority and formulate a set of principles.[53] It's not enough to have an identity[54] from which to enter the world; we must behave consistent with values, principles and integrity.[55] January 8th the birthday of dynamic strength. One that is born

---

[48] HK of the M. H. T. of S 1927 p. 3 "Dear Mothers, teach these lessons to your little ones, that they may learn to love instead of hate." Also chapter 3 Elihu's lessons-The Unity Of Life

[49] Moorish Literature are Excerpts taken from the Moorish Guide 1927-1928 What is Islam? Object of man's life. According to Islam, is its complete unfoldment. Islam teaches that man is born with unlimited capacities for progress.

[50] Prophet Noble Drew Ali was 29 years old in the year of 1915 the following next year of 1916 he started the Moorish National and Divine Movement.

[51] Moorish Literature are Excerpts taken from the Moorish Guide 1927-1928 p. 10 What is Islam? "The goal of a man's life, according to Islam, is peace with everything. Peace with ALLAH and peace with man."

[52] Prophet Noble Drew Ali's message was to Know Thyself and ALLAH.

[53] From The Divine Constitution And By-Laws of the M.H.T of S Act 3- Love, Truth, Peace, Freedom and Justice must be proclaimed and practiced.

[54] Ibid. Act 6- With us all members must proclaim their nationality. (Moorish American)

[55] Moorish Literature are Excerpts taken from the Moorish Guide 1927-1928 p. 14 Moorish Leader's Historical Message To America " I most anxiously hope this brief statement will help you to more clearly see the duty and wisdom of at all times upholding those fundamental principles which are desired for our civilization of our posterity, such as obedience to law, respect and loyalty to government, tolerance, and unity."

on this date always make their presence felt.[56] They are meant to shine and, with their inspired awareness, inner strength and self-discipline with a stunning potential to rise and shine above all obstacles and make an impact on the world around them. Whatever career these people choose, they tend to rise to the top, be it in the sciences, business or humanitarian work. They have an ability to communicate,[57] teach[58] and inspire[59] others may lead them to education,[60] spirituality,[61] medicine[62] and philosophy.[63] The life path of people born on this day is to rise above the odds. Once they have developed[64] their communication skills and ability to put others at their ease, their destiny is to show others that the possibilities are always there and that if they are positive and put in the necessary hard work they will be victorious. There are those who see Noble Drew Ali's image, and there are those, who has felt his spiritual presences. The man behind the image and the voice that speaks within. He came 48 years after the emancipation of

---

[56] Ibid. Savior of Humanity Losing all sight on those things worldly and yielding absolutely to a cause higher than has ever yet been attained. This picture is the likeness of Prophet Noble Drew Ali, who is serving humanity.

[57] HK of the M. H. T. of S 1927 Chap. 26-V2 "Hath He endowed thee with wisdom? Hath He enlightened thy mind with the knowledge of truth? Communicate it to the ignorant, for their instruction; communicate it to the wise, for thine own improvement."

[58] From The Divine Constitution And By-Laws of the M.H.T of S Act 6- We are teaching our people their Nationality.

[59] Moorish Literature are Excerpts taken from the Moorish Guide 1927-1928 Moorish Leader's Historical Message To America " Brighten the hopes of our youth in order that their courage be increased to dare and do wondrous things."

[60] Education is when you truly learn about yourself.

[61] HK of the M. H. T. of S 1927 Chap. 37-V10 Keep thy soul in moderation; teach thy spirit to attentive to its good; so shall these, its ministers be always to thee conveyances of truth.

[62] Prophet Noble Drew Ali was the founder of the Moorish Manufacturing Corp. (He made Moorish Tea, a body builder and blood purifier. Moorish Healing Oil and Moorish Antiseptic Bath Compound).

[63] HK of the M. H. T. of S 1927 Chap. 26-V10 "The attainment of virtue he accounteth as the highest learning; and the science of happiness is the study of his life."

[64] Ibid. chap. 48-V1 "The last Prophet in these days is Noble Drew Ali, who was prepared divinely in due time by ALLAH."

1865 and the **Moorish Holy Koran**[65] of 1927 which provided us with 48 chapters of words of wisdom. By this time Noble Drew Ali has given us our proclamation. The awakening words from the echoes of the past "The fallen sons and daughters of the Asiatic Nation of North America need to learn to love instead of hate" from these words you can feel the passion of love coming from the fountain of his heart for the benefit of humanity. He has assisted the poor in their trouble. He promotes peace and love in their hearts and let us say for the record of life that the real man within is the true essence of his spirit. Noble Drew Ali has raised the consciousness of people who were enslaved mentally. What is the story behind this man of whom we await;[66] Let us turn back the pages of time with a open mind. Timothy Drew lost his mother when he was very young, just before she past away it was said that she knew that her son will be a great leader. If you know like I know that our mother's words carry an impact of our lives. We will have to say that his father past before his mother. Life expectancy for males during that early 16 to 17 century was very short. As a child Timothy hold a Great Spirit unlike any other child.[67] And so ALLAH who had prepared the form in advance for the great work he was to do when he reached manhood. Timothy spent his younger life traveling with a Gypsy[68] group. While with the Gypsy's, Timothy was blamed for a theft

---

[65] The Moorish Holy Koran is known as the Circle Seven. The description of this was written in the Holy Bible in Revelation chapter 5 And I saw in the right hand of him that sat on the throne a book written within and on the backside, sealed with seven seals.

[66] This is very interesting , when Noble Drew Ali started out in the year of 1913, there also was a book out that same year it is called Cosmic Consciousness The Man-God Whom we await by Ali Nomad. This book contains examples of cosmic consciousness who have founded new systems of religion, Moses, Gautama (Buddha) Jesus of Nazareth, and Mohammed. Dr. Alexander Mcivor-Tyndall a hypnotist adopted the pseudonym name Nomad Ali. There is no information on how he obtain this information.

[67] HK of the M. H. T. of S 1927 Chap. 5- V9 " Do you know that I must be about my Father's work?"

[68] The Gypsies, then, whom we have already seen described as "Moors," were also "Saracens." p. 140 taken from the book Ancient and Modern Britons Vol. I 1884 by David Macritche. The Saracen are the descendants of Abraham's wife Sara. Saracen which means sons of Sara. Gypsies - E gypsies - Egyptians

in the camp.[69] An old Gypsy women[70] came to his defense and he was later cleared of the charges. Little did we know that history in some ways repeats it self. And so it did, Prophet Noble Drew Ali has been accused of copying the Moorish circle 7 Holy Koran from the 1907 **Aquarian Gospel of Jesus the Christ by Levi.**[71] But did Levi copied this Gospel? In 1894 Nicolas Notovich[72] published a book called **The Unknown Life of Christ.** It is also worth mentioning that a man name James Churchward[73] had written a book called **"The Children of Mu**[74]**"** in Chapter 16 "Intimate hours with the Rishi" James Churchward said:

> "A record copy in the Himis Monastery at Leh, Kashmir, that states " When Jesus left his home country, he first went to Egypt

---

[69] He was accused of stealing a book.

[70] During our cultural times we had the utmost respect for our elders, especially from the words of our wisest woman. When she speaks the world listens.

[71] Levi H. Dowling a Scotch Welsh descendent Born May 18, 1844 passed August 13, 1911 it was said that he gain this information from the Akashic Records in which the mind of man is in exact accord with the Universal Mind man so it my enter into a conscious recognition of these Akashic impressions, so it collect them and translate them into any language of earth. One must take notice that there is evidence of Moorish presence in Scotland and England as early as the tenth century. " Ivan Van Sertima Golden age of the Moor. P. 339" Therefore Levi had taken some information from the Moors and not from the Akashic records.

[72] Nicolas Notovitch was a Russian doctor who journeyed through Tibet, he had an accident that resulted in his leg being broken. While there, he was being ministered at the Himis convent. He learned that there existed ancient records of Jesus. It was known as "The Life of St. Issa." Notovitch had a Tibetan translate Two large volumes of the biography of St. Issa. To prove the original Tibetan documents existed. Swami Adhedananda journeyed to Himis and found that it was true . And he wrote a book also entitled Kashmir O Tibetti. In 1925 another Russian named Nicholas Roerich saw the same documents and he recorded in his own travel diary the same biography of St. Issa.

[73] James Churchward was a British born occult writer who befriended a Indian priest, the priest disclosed the existence of several ancient tablets of the lost Continent of Mu with its history, inhabitants and Sciences.

[74] The Continent Mu or Lemuria which was located North of Hawaii to the South as far as Fijis and Easter Island. This 1931 book The lost Continent of Mu had stated that the Spaniards who invaded and conquered South America came from the south of Spain where everything partook of Moorish atmosphere and they themselves were half Moors in all of their conceptions. p. 86

and was there for two years studied the ancient Osirian religion. From Egypt he went to India and many cities, including Benares and Lahore, he studied the teachings of Gautama Buddha. After this he entered a Himalayan monastery where for 12 years he studied the Sacred Inspired writings of Mu the Motherland, and her Cosmic Sciences. At the end of 12 years he became a master."

For a moment let us return back to Nicholas Notovitch, he became a hated man from the orthodox Muslims and Christians because of the Jesus in India theory. Finally there is a conformation of accuracy of the scriptures about Jesus from seven[75] visitor's who went to Himis and saw the documents of Jesus. Noble Drew Ali's pamphlet[76] of 1927 stated "The genealogy of Jesus with eighteen years of the events, life, works and teachings in India, Europe and Africa" From 1886 in North Carolina until 1913 Newark N.J. Where was Noble Drew Ali during a time be- tween time. Timothy was thinking of going to Egypt to continue his search for truth. When the future Prophet was alone one day, A voice had said, " If you go, I will follow." He did not except it at first until the third time. He left the Gypsy camp, never to return. When Timothy was in the East, in every way of life he would walk, in every hall of learning he would sit; the heights that any man has gained, these he would gain.[77] Timothy went down into the dismal crypts[78] and pass the hardest of tests.[79] Timothy entered into the

---

[75] Nicholas Notovitch 1887 saw document - Swami Abhedananda 1922 saw document - Nicholas Roerich and son 1925 saw document - Mrs. Gasque and Madame Caspari 1939 saw document - Dr. R. Ravicz 1973 Oral reference: informed by an Tibetan friend U. Eichstadt 1974 saw document.

[76] HK of the M. H. T. of S 1927 p. 3 "All authority and rights of publishing of this pamphlet of 1927."

[77] Ibid. Chap. 13 V12

[78] There is a tunnel under Giza. No one knows when it was constructed or how. An expedition was mounted as result of data gathered back in the 1920's and 1930's about a secret chamber under the pyramid. They built equipment in later years and went in down into the pyramid and found this metal door 500 feet below the base of the pyramid. They found other doors. This information was taken from Hard Truth Wake up America www. theforbiddenknowledge.com/ hard truth/pyramids index.htm

[79] HK of the M. H. T. of S 1927 Chap. 13-V14

school of the Prophet's, he learned and studied the life of Jesus and sacred lessons of Know Thyself. The future prophet knew just what our people needed in America, but before he can teach us, he must wake up those who need it the most and they were called the negroes and black people. For they have been dehumanize under the iron hand oppression of those who have no mercy in them. Prophet Noble Drew Ali was guided by ALLAH to free us from an European concept of Christianity,[80] in which it was founded in Rome for their earthly salvation. You may disagree, but this is not intended to offend anyone in any way, what I am asking is for you to have an open mind and read without prejudice. Like Nicholas Notovitch the Prophet was mis- understood and hated by the Christians.[81] From the **Moorish Guide**[82] "Religious Controversy", Ali's words express his concerns in the matter of faith and truth, he said: **"The fact of the matter is that they have always had only a reflection of the truth and not the real thing"**.

What Ali give us was the truth about Jesus[83] that he learned and studied from the Egyptian school. Naturally doth man desire the truth, because carnal man want not the truth; they love falsehood of darkness, and when the light of truth shines in the dark they comprehend it not. Behold, truth breedeth hatered. The fault is not in truth, for that is amiable, but the weakness of man. Ali had challenge us to take a look at our weakness and at our own ignorance, without hatered. That is why he made this known in the inside and backside cover of the Moorish Holy Koran, he stated:

> **"That you may learn to love instead of hate"**

---

[80] Ibid. Chap. 46 The Beginning of Christianity

[81] Moorish Literature are Excerpts taken from the Moorish Guide 1927-1928 Moorish Leader's Historical Message To America the Prophet said: "The M. H. T of S has received some opposition and criticism. In the main, the opposition has come from certain Christian ministers. They have expressed themselves as being opposed to our propagation of the of the religion of Islam."

[82] Ibid. Religious Controversy

[83] HK of the M. H. T. of S 1927 Chap. 46-V2 Jesus himself was of the true blood of the ancient Canaanites and Moabites and the inhabitants of Africa.

What Ali was revealing to America was just the opposite of what the Christians were promoting. We were given a false image[84] with a false doctrine of a religion that enslaves you. Just like all other Prophets before him, he came to correct the falsehood that was used by Satan,[85] because Satan deceived the people with his cunning ways. Also the Muslims rejected Ali's prophethood and the **Moorish Holy Koran**. By the late 1920's a Sudanese missionary came to the United States and there was an encounter, direct or indirect between Noble Drew Ali and Satti Majid Muhammad al-Qadi of Dongola. Satti says that he wrote to Noble Drew Ali and advised him to change his name and burn his book. Satti continues by saying that he attempted to take Ali to court to seek American justice and put the latter to the test.[86] He wanted Ali to prove his Prophethood by performing miracles.[87] Ali's clam was reviewed by specialist in African American Islam, upon their evaluation they said: as a Sharif,[88] he did

---

[84] Remember this, "who ever controls image's controls your mind."

[85] Satan- meaning adversary. Metaphysical meaning- The deceiving phase of mind in man that has fixed ideas in opposition to truth. M. H. T. of S Questionary 74 Where are you going Satan? I am going to and fro the earth seeking whom I may devour.

[86] HK of the M. H. T. of S 1927 Chap. 15-V7 "Who is it that demands a test?

[87] Ibid. Chap. 15 "It is no sign that one is a prophet of ALLAH because he does a miracle; the devils can do mighty things."

[88] Sharif means Noble, this also brings an enlightening discovery The original 13th Article of Amendment. Remember that Noble Drew Ali begin in the year 1913. The original 13th Article of Amendment, ratified in 1819 and just disappeared in 1876, In January, 1810, Senator Reed proposed the "Title of Nobility" and "honor." On April 27, 1810, the Senate voted to pass this 13th Amendment by a vote of 26 to 1. No record has been found that the State of Connecticut ever acted to either accept or reject this original 13th Amendment. Yet, it was published in three separate editions of "The Public Statute Laws of the State of Connecticut" as part of the U.S. Constitution in 1821, 1824 and 1835. Then, without record or explanation, it mysteriously disappeared from subsequent editions prior to the Civil War between the states. It appeared in a manual printed in 1840 for American citizen. Some words printed on the front cover that read. The American citizens Manual of Reference: UNITED STATES OF NORTH AMERICA. And of the Several States and Territories Front and back Seals with the Eagle and pyramid First, "Titles of Nobility" were prohibited in both Article VI of the Articles of Confederation (1777) and in Article I, section 9 and 1of the Constitution of the United States (1787) The missing 13th Amendment to The Constitution of the United States reads as follows: If any citizen of the United States shall accept, clam, receive, or retain any title nobility or

proclaim a new revelation out of Morocco[89] the land of the Moors, and did claimed to have traveled and been with the ulama of various Muslim countries.[90] In other words, on the basis of what we know about Ali's doctrinal position, the charges, from Satti's perspective, was not false. The response from the Middle East is equally difficult to evaluate. One interpretation is to view the various fatwa that Satti obtained as essentially routine documents. The problem with this is that there would be a prophet in the U.S.A in the late 1920's could hardly have been a routine designation. Again, we are in the dark.[91] There is the story that Satti was prevented from returning

---

honor, or shall without the consent of Congress, accept and retain any present, pension, office, or emolument of any kind whatever, from any Emperor, King, Prince, or foreign power, such person shall cease to be a citizen of the United States, and shall be incapable of holding any office of trust or profit under them, or either of them. Just a theory of a thought that may be of future reference. There is also another 13 amendment, it is known as the 13-20. Which has the missing 20 sections. Let it be known that Noble Drew Ali was born a Noble from the Cherokee nation.

[89] The last Sultan of Morocco was Glaoui Pasha "Hadj Thami El-Glaoui"(1893-1956) " The Black Panther" of Morocco. He was the most power figure in Morocco during his lifetime. World's Great Men of Color 1946 J.A. Rogers p. 405 The Sultan of Morocco recognize Noble Drew Ali's Nobility.

[90] Arabia is another country that recognize Noble Drew Ali's Nobility from Sultan Abdul Aziz Ibn Suad. With this thought in mind "the door to Moorish mysteries is opening far and wide" these are the words From the Montauk Book of the Dead by peter Moon he goes on to say The age of Pisces is at an end, and the Moors are coming to receive their inheritance. In 1928, The Noble Prophet attended a Pan American conference in Havana Cuba where he enjoyed broad recognition from a host of other countries. They were , of course, recognizing his sovereign status as a Moorish national who was representing the ancient empire of Amexem. (In a closed meeting) Ali received a document which was to change the face of Moorish Nation forever and would eventually lead to what is known as the Great Schism. The document Drew Ali received was a copy of a mandate whereby the Amexem Empire extended a land grant of the entire Western Hemisphere to certain Europeans. The unseen document and its contents are highly mysterious. (within this close room withheld the words of the Prophet) before Ali left he placed 4 stakes into Cuba's soil to protect the land. Several heads of state held a conference in Geneva, Switzer-land between several nations about the mandate that Ali had given them. Series of discussions and negotiations , records are still kept sealed to this very day. Ali had told the Moors to get their money out of the banks. Why? It was the crash of 1929. United States, Portugal, France, and Spain, declared bankruptcy. You may be thinking who is this man? He is Prophet Noble Drew Ali.

[91] What is applied here is that they do not have an answer to Satti's claim.

to the States because he seems to have been perceived by the FBI as a potential ally of Japan. Having failed to gain Al-Azhar's approval and being seemingly prevented from returning to America. Satti returned to the Sudan sometime in the 1940 and died there March 17, 1963. One must keep in mind that if Satti was correct with his accusation, then why did other Muslims came to support him or prove his point to America. Storms roar against his shoulders but are not able to shake them; the thunder burst over his head in vain; lightning serveth but to show the glories of his countenance. His name is Prophet Noble Ali ! His eye[92] discover the Moorish Temple beyond the limits of time. He enter in it boldly, and he remain there forever. You see, he is the **Moorish Holy Temple**.[93] **The Moorish Holy Koran** also has another portion of teachings. Its source was a book call "Unto Thee I Grant" a 1925 mystical book published by the Ancient Mystical Order Rosae Crucis[94] (AMORC) The doctrines of this book were from Tibet,[95] or was it? There is every indication throughout the words of **"Unto Thee Thy Grant"** the amazing wisdom was written by Amenhotep IV, Pharaoh of Egypt,[96] during the years of 1360 to 1350 B.C. He was

---

[92] Noble Drew Ali said that I am the Eagle stirring in the nest (the nest was America) In Shamanism the Eagle represent the East, the Eagle means mental clarity, their element is air, and they can see beyond vision, wings elevated display rising. If you look very closely on our Moorish Divine Constitution and by Laws you will see Ali wearing a robe and tie you will see within the tie a eagle The knot of the tie is the eagles head and the collar is the wings. This was an old version sketch of an eagle (you can also look on page 13 on his flyer.)

[93] Moorish Literature are excerpts taken from the Moorish Guide 1927-1928 p.18 Divine Warning By The Prophet Noble Drew Ali "If the prophet is not right, the temple is not right."

[94] Today it is known as The Rosicrucian Order. (Rose Cross) its founder C.R.C. a German born man who was pursuing the studies of the secrets of the Arabian adepts in the city of Damcar. After three years in Damcar, he departed for the city of Fez in Morocco where his interest was of the Moorish Sciences. After two years in Fez, C.R.C. sailed for Spain. Where the Moors of Spain had left a vast knowledge of their Sciences. C.R.C. was schooled by Moorish Science.

[95] The Grand Lama claimed that the manuscript had been in their teachings since 732 A.D. It may have been in the possession of some Adepts and Masters outside of Tibet for many years before that date.

[96] Let it be known once again that Prophet Noble Drew Ali journey into Egyptland and

the first to proclaim the belief in one Creator He established the Secret Brotherhood and the true author of the hundred and fourth Psalm, and many sacred writings of the East have been definitely traced to his school and Brotherhood. There were also the schools of the Essenes[97] to which the Master Jesus belonged to. Written on the walls of time of the entrance of the scared school was "Know Thyself" Prophet Noble Drew Ali was a Master[98] man. He left some very important information in his works, words and deeds. he said:

"Read carefully the doctrines of The Moorish Holy Temple of Science. It contains our hopes, aims, rules and articles of religion."[99]

On the front of the **Moorish Divine Constitution and by-laws**, The Prophet left a visual message in which it reveals the title of the name of a Scared Adept book. The author's name was given from a statement

---

was received as a pupil in the school of the Prophets, where Jesus and John once attend.

[97] The Essenes considered their Brotherhood-Sisterhood as the presence on earth of teaching of the sons and daughters of the Universal Creator. They possessed their advanced knowledge and worked in secret for the triumph of the light over the darkness of the human mind. They were not limited to a single religion, but studied all of them in order to extract the great scientific principles. They considered each religion to be a different stage of a single revelation. The Essenes accorded great importance to the teachings of ancient Chaldeans, of Prophet Zoroaster, of hermes trismegiste, to the secret instructions of Moses and one of the founding Masters of their order who had transmitted techniques similar to those of Buddhism, as well as to the revelation of Enoch. They possessed a living science of all of these revelations. All Brothers and 15 Sisters wore white. The Hebrews called them "The School of prophets", and to the Egyptians, They were "The Healers, The Doctors." Take note of John "The Baptist" father, was a minister of the Essenes.

[98] HK of the M. H. T. of S 1927 Chap. 4-V16 The teacher treads the way; on every span of ground he leaves his foot-prints, clearly cut, which all can see and be assured that he, their master, went that way.

[99] Moorish Literature are Excerpts taken from the Moorish Guide 1927-1928 Moorish Leader's Historical Message To America. Now remember that the word religion means to unite again (to think) which was lost.

from Brother John Givens El[100] for the sole purpose of protecting the Prophet's movement. This book was published in the eighteen hundreds before **"Unto Thee I Grant"** The scared lessons of life that Prophet Noble Drew Ali had obtained in the School of the Prophets and his journeying in foreign lands; and about the meetings he had with the masters. Coming back home to America to deliver the truth about man. With the under- standing about true love you may witness a Prophet, you will see clearly of all things that seems to be, if you are more open minded to life as it truly is and realize the only reality is ALLAH. (You reveal of what you think by how you are dress) It is said a picture is worth a thousand words and if we look at what the Prophet wore in some of his photos he gives us some eye opening information about himself and his history. For example there are two photo's of the Prophet sitting on a chair, this chair is representing sitting on a throne[101] a living symbol of his position and his authority. Wearing a white turban with an eagle's feather[102] which means a divine spirit with a clear vision. He is also wearing a daisy, the history of the daisy can be trace back to the Sacred Symbols of Mu and Atlantis. It repre-

---

[100] Brother John Givens El was a well known Adept with a clean heart of mind, (Thru the will of ALLAH) of whom he spiritually absorbed Prophet Noble Drew Ali's teaching. This was called by the Prophet himself before he past form, that he will return Spiritually. (Reincarnation) his knowledge of his teachings.

[101] The Throne is the order of Angel s ranking after the Seraphim and Cherubim. This is one who belong to the first and highest triad of heavenly host. This position makes them some of the most powerful angels in the service of ALLAH. The question is, what is our Prophet to us? He is an Angel of ALLAH. (Us simply means those who are spiritually awaken, who knows that Noble Drew Ali is the one that was sent by ALLAH) One that sits on a Throne has the status of sovereign power of the first sphere of the third order. They are the keepers of the higher more expanded energies. ALLAH'S Spirit is conveyed in a certain manner to these angels, who in turn pass on message to men. (Noble Drew Ali was to carry messages to the nations thus saying to bring us the Everlasting Gospel.)

[102] An Eagle Feather symbolizes trust, honor, strength, wisdom, power and freedom. If any Moorish Cherokee is given a Golden or Bold Eagle feathers it is one of the most rewarding items they can ever be handed. Our Moorish nations or tribes believe that eagles have a special connection with the heavens since they fly so close. Many believe that if they are given this feather, it is a symbol from above. They believe that there is a spiritual power in feathers and it provides protection. He was also given an ostrich feather- which means a well grounded and practical person. This goes back to The Dogon people of Mali & Kemet.

sent the sun and her rays. It is also known as the sunflower. The radiation the sunflower carries, will help you to develop a higher consciousness. You may notice that he is wearing a sash[103] across his right shoulder, keep this in mind that the Shaman Medicine[104] man always carry a medicine bag.[105] The first photo of Noble Drew Ali as the Egyptian Adept, he was wearing a white robe[106] with a sash around his waist.

---

[103] Sash is a symbol of sealing power and authority with love. Also it displays a position of president.

[104] Prophet Noble Drew Ali was the founder of the Moorish Manufacturing Company, He produce the Moorish Oil, Moorish Compound and Moorish Tea. All products were made from herbs for healing the human form. It may be of interest to read a book "The Sacred formulas of the Cherokees", 1886 by James Mooney read selected list of plants used.

[105] A medicine bag is an ancient item that spiritually represents the person who wears it. The reason to carry a medicine are for guidance, healing and protection. By wearing it close to you, you are connecting with your spiritual self, the authentic you and always remembering who you are.

[106] Prophet Zoroaster of Persia (now Iran) wears a white turban and white robe and sash. The sacred book was "Zen Avesta" his teaching was the doctrines of individual judgment of Heaven and Hell (state of mind). And the Resurrection of the body. These teachings became the lessons of Jesus . HK of the M.H.T of S. Chapter 11 Jesus and Barata- Together they read the sacred books V2 "Together Jesus and read the Jewish Psalms and prophets, read the Vedas, the Avesta and the wisdom of Guatama."

After Noble Drew Ali announced his Prophet hood in **1925**. He made an historic trip to Washington, D.C. The president at that time was Calvin Coolidge.[107] The Prophet made diplomatic maneuvers to see the President.

---

[107] Calvin Coolidge 1872 -1933. Mothers maiden name was "Moor" she was born 1846 Vermont Victoria Josephine Moor. President Coolidge pardoned Marcus Garvey from the government mail fraud scam in 1927. Note: Noble Drew Ali had visited Mr. Garvey at the Federal Prison in Atlanta Ga. on Oct. 23. 1927.

Unlike other so called black leaders Prophet Noble Drew Ali did not ask for Civil rights,[108] he asked for Divine Rights,[109] (highest authority in the land), to call his people[110] and teach the principles of their ancient forefathers. The Prophet asked for the names and nationality which was taken away from the Moors back in the year 1779. The President told the Prophet that he will give him that right, but he also said:

"As long as they keep their schools and churches open, you won't get ten to follow you"

Prophet's reply:

"The sheep knows the shepherd's voice."

The Prophet continue to move for the development of the Moorish Nation by going into the secret vaults in Washington, D.C. where the European officials for one-hundred and forty-six years had the secrets of the Moors of Northwest Africa hidden. In the old flag book, the green star, was missing from the Moorish flag.[111] The prophet told the European

---

[108] Moorish Literature are Excerpts taken from the Moorish Guide 1927-1928 A Divine Warning By The Prophet For The Nations "Through the Moorish Divine National Movement our children can receive their Divine rights, unmolested by other citizens that they can cast a free national ballot to the pools under the free national constitution of the States Government and not under a granted privilege as has been the existing condition for many generations" Civil rights are for convicts and slaves.

[109] Human Rights. French Declaration of Human Rights (1789). Declaration of the Rights of the child (1924).

[110] It was said that President Coolidge had said: "what people?" The Prophet said "those who you call negro, black and colored" It was also said that the President said: " Why should I give you the right to teach and who are you to ask a sure question?" The Prophet reply : "I am ALLAH'S representative" then the Prophet had demonstrated before the eyes of the President something that he will never forget. At this time the President had acknowledged of who this man was.

[111] Moorish Koran Questionary Q18 What kind of flag is the Moorish? It is a red flag with a five pointed green star in the center. This flag went down July 4, 1776 by George Washington. By being defeated as a nation and to erase our Moorish history this was told as a story that George Washington cutting down a cherry tree (the Moorish flag was red

officials to return it. This was the Moorish oldest flag, it was called **"Old Glory'** Prophet Noble Drew Ali said it is over 10.000 years old. I guess you are wondering by now, that this flag is the same as Morocco.[112] But Morocco did not have this flag until later on after the late twenties.[113] And Morocco did not get its independence from France until March 2, 1956. Again who is this man with so much knowledge of our Moorish flag and who could of known these events of our Moorish illustrious history. Prophet Noble Drew Ali was the best kept secret that this U.S. government was trying to hide for many years[114], since his return back to America from Egypt. His return was at Norfolk VA. When he arrived, they were trying to deport him until he gave them papers stating that he was from America. What ever said between the European officials and the prophet. It lead him to be detained, and they questioned him on his purpose for being here. The Prophet said I came for my people, the officials said leave those people alone and we will release you. The Prophet looked on with a stern face and said with power

---

as a cherry) In the year of 1816 Fort Mosa which was called by the Europeans as Fort Negro in Florida. Before being the President a slave owner General Andrew Jackson Demanded to demolish Fort Mosa. It was said Jackson's gunboats sailing up the river, while being on the bluff they spotted the Mosa Fort. A red flag was above the fort. Noble Drew Ali demanded that the star was to be place on our flag. The star was the true star of David and the official seal of Jerusalem 300, c150 BC. The five points represent ALLAH, look at the limbs of man Arm-Leg-Leg-Arm-Head this is recorded in the King James version of the Bible Revelations 3:12 "Him that overcometh will I make a pillar in the temple of my God, And he shall go no more out: and I will write upon him the name of my God." This is ALLAH.

[112] The Arabic name for Morocco is al-Maghrib al-aqsa which means " The Extreme West " also Mauritania was the name of Morocco in the 8th century A.D. Morocco was one of the kingdoms of the Moorish Empire. One thought in mind if our Moorish flag was raised here in the U.S.A., how did Morocco obtained the same flag?

[113] In fact this was not always the Moroccan flag in the year of 1884 to 1913. From the flag chart of the nations the Moroccan Flag displayed two swords crossed with a red field and white border. It look like two scissors, and if you really want more insight this flag was on several flag charts It is reported on Dutch flag charts as (Moorse flag Moorish flag); later it became Moroccan flag. This was also known as the Ottoman Empire flag During the 16th and the 17th centuries. Look up Ottoman Empire: flags with Zulfika and Morocco Historical flags this will share some light.

[114] From the statements and Prophesies of Noble Drew Ali he said " If you don't be careful, 50 years after I am gone, you want know that I have been here."

and authority "Never! Never! no more to Rome" the officials took the bed mattress away from Ali and left. Later on they came back and ask him again to leave those people alone. And again Ali said" Never! Never! no more to Rome" At this time they have taken away the cart that the mattress was on. Ali had to rest on a cold floor, and this is where his health problems begin, for many years from Newark N.J to Chicago ILL. He upheld his form until 1929.[115]

With an open mind one must realize that we are spiritual beings having human experiences. Noble Drew Ali's spirit was an exceptional, he had to be, because his mission was to bring our people out of darkness into a marvelous light,[116] and give the world the truth about man and his true GOD This is the reason why ALLAH the Great GOD of the universe ordained Noble Drew Ali the Prophet to redeem his people from their sinful ways. The dignity of his character was well known, for when a man act that is him. Noble Drew Ali promoted much more then what we imaged. You see the mind of man is the cause both of his bondage and of his liberation. A wise man cultivates his mind with knowledge he feeleth his imperfections and is humbled. Nevertheless, the attainment of virtue he accouteth as the highest learning; and the science of happiness is the study of his life. Here is to the man of spirit and soul of love, bound to this earth with a remedy for the minds that became mental slaves. A young boy who lost his mother, and witness discrimination at a time that was full of hatred from those who has no mercy in them. A compassionate man, a true seer in a prophet, who lives in the higher spiritual (firmaments.) Whose octaves

---

[115] The certificate of death Noble Drew Ali had rest his form Saturday, July 20, 1929 at 9:50pm the cause of death was Tuberculosis Bronchitis Pneumonia. At his bedside were his private physician Dr. Clarence Payne-El, Attorney Aaron Payne-El, his father in-law, Foreman -Bey and wife, Mary Drew. The U.S history record states that 100 years ago the number one death in America was Pneumonia. Note* the law officials of Chicago in 1929 did the same thing to him as it was done in Norfolk Va.

[116] Uncovering the European U.S. government conspiracy . In the House of Delegates of Virginia, in 1832, A senator by the name of Henry Berry said: "We have as far as possible closed every avenue by which the LIGHT will enter the SLAVES MIND. If we could extinguish the capacity to see the LIGHT our work would be complete. They would then be on the level with the beast of the field. And we would be safe.

of vibration is at the very realm of Love, He who gives understandingly, teaches, he who receives with comprehension, learns. Therefore, if man can communicate it to the ignorant, for their instruction and communicate to the wise, for their own improvement. He can instruct, but not alone by words. To conceive correctly or to come to a full sense of realization, three factors are necessary, knowledge, the knower, and the known. The Universal Creator ALLAH can only be known Spiritually. The object of these pages in which the very light of heaven may be reflected in the form of a man as we known as Noble Drew Ali. The man of whom we await to bring us the cosmic consciousness of the sciences of "Know Thyself."

CHAPTER II

THE MOOR

PROPHET Noble Drew Ali said: **"It will take you 50 years to find out what I brought you"** Probably the first time we have seen a so-called black[117] man and the word Moor together, was on the cover of a book called "The story of the Moors in Spain" by Stanley Lane-Poole.[118] 1886 the same year that Noble Drew Ali was born. Ali said that we are the descendants of the ancient Moabites[119] who inhabited the Northwestern and South western shores of Africa.[120] Ali was also a Moorish historian,

---

[117] Moorish Koran Questionary Q 87 What is meant by the word Black? Black according to science means death. What this simply means is that black in science carry's a lower vibration. The color symbolism plays an important part in the shamanistic system of the Cherokees. Each one of the cardinal points has its corresponding color and each color its symbolic meaning, so that each spirit invoked corresponds in color and local habitation with the characteristics imputed to him, and is connected with other spirits of the same name. Which explains why Black means death. And from the science of symbol's B represent life and death, when the symbol B is applied with the other symbol's LACK it will attach its lower spiritual attributes to the subject who proclaims that they are Black (you must remember this may take form in finite or infinite point of view) Finite view is your understanding of self, infinite is your spiritual wisdom of self. Question 90 Can a man be a Negro, Black , Colored or Ethiopian? No.

[118] The author Stanley Edward Lane-Poole, was born in London on December 18, 1854. He studied Oriental and Egyptology.

[119] Moabites were the seeds of Moab the grandson of Lot. The story of Lot in the King James version was untrue. Lot was not the father of Moab. Once again ALLAH has given use a Prophet to correct Satan's lies, this time it was Prophet Mohammed (PBUH) He gave us The Holy Quran, This was done because of the falsehood of the Bible by man. The record here has evidently been manipulated. Abraham, who was his Uncle, considered Lot a righteous servant. The Holy Quran by Maulana Muhammad Ali 7th edition. The science of the name Moabites which means thoughts springing from and belonging to that in conscious -ness which Moab signifies.

[120] M. H. T. of S The Divine Constitution And By-Laws Act.6

he made a eye opening statement "What your ancient forefathers were, you are today without doubt or contradiction." Ask yourself this question, would you trust or believe in someone that has taken away your birthrights, enslaved[121] your forefathers to believe in their concept of religion[122] and to make law,[123] to enforce the people to be obedient to that law. This brings us to this statement:

> **"Who controls the past, controls the future. Who controls the present, controls the past." By George Orwell, 1984**

The first generation of slaves was physically bond in chains only, mentally, they were free. The Moors[124] knew who they were and where they came from. As our ancestors are calling us like ancient winds of time, and with your undivided attention we will journey back in time and see what our true Moorish history will reveal to us. In the 8th century A.D. the Moors recaptured Spain and took with them, the wisdom teaching or Mysteries of Egypt.[125] From this, Spain became the center of all learning

---

[121] A slave not being regarded as a member of Society, nor as a human being, The slave is a "chattel" his master is his owner, just like he owns cattle's. A slave is property and his master can do anything to their property . Sell, beat, rape and even kill you.

[122] Religion means government principles, law and order. (A religion that put you into slavery cannot save you from slavery).

[123] Here are just some of the many laws that were placed on the Moors of America. The State of VA fugitive Law Authorized branding of an "R" in the Face of runaway slaves 1667 Slavery legalized Baptism did not change the status of the convert, meaning Christian slaves would remain enslaved.1775- VA running Law allowed sale or execution of slaves attempting to flee 1787- The U.S. Constitution states that Congress may not ban the slave trade until 1808 and counts every slave as three-fifths of a person1819- Missouri literacy Law forbade assembling or teaching black slaves to read or write. 1848- VA incitement Law provided death penalty for advising slaves to read 1857- U.S Supreme Court rules in case of Dred Scott that slaves are private property and cannot become U.S citizens.

[124] They knew that they were not Black people, Negroes, and or blackamoor name by the Europeans.

[125] During these times an earlier the secret schools of Egypt (Kemet) were neither fraternal nor political fundamentally, nor were there similar to those of the modern Craft. Once these teachings were in the hands of the European Nations they began to change its

in the world. In fact Moorish history was known as the Golden Age. When Europe was still in its complete darkness of knowledge, the Moors of Spain became a cultural and intellectual Mecca where scared manuscripts and texts were collected and translated. Cities such as Cordoba, Seville and Granda had public and private gardens. Public hospitals were Moorish physicians had texts written for surgical procedures, public baths with hot and cold running water. From the pages of J.A. Rogers[126] 1952 "Nature Know no Color Line" he said:

> **"Seven years after the capture of Spain the Moors invaded France. In 837 they captured Sicily. In 846, they invaded Italy, seized Rome. Thereafter they dominated most of Italy for years and parts of it until the thirteenth century. In Africa the Moors continued to be a leading power, and to no little extent in India, also. They dominated the Mediterranean and the North Atlantic and plundered the coast of Western Europe and the British Isles. They even conquered and ruled parts of Scotland."[127]**

This clearly will show you that these nations became part of the Moorish Empire, so when Ali said that we are descendants or Moroccans and born in American.[128] "He was letting us know that no matter where we were from, we were descendants of the people of many lands, that was of Moorish descent. Or if you were an Moroccan from Morocco you

---

main objective (rule by the compass and the square). Which mean control the land by the compass and to do it by force with the square (weapons).

[126] Joel Augustus Rogers was born in Nigril Jamaica September 6, 1883 or 1888 He moved to the U.S. in 1906 in Harlem NY. Between 1925 and 1927 he researched in Europe and North Africa. With the blessing of our Father ALLAH without school learning in this field. His research in libraries, museums and anthropologists. He was known as a prolific writer as a historian and Journalist. He was Gods gift to America (This was also the name of one of his great books, 1961). During his travels J.A. Rogers was fully aware of the Moorish Movement in America.

[127] Ibid, p. 69 - this book contains Moors in the coats of Arms of Noble Families of French, German, and Dutch (Truly a must read).

[128] Koran Questionary, question 14 Why are we Moorish Americas? Moorish by descendant and American by birth.

was still be known as Moorish. Europe in the 15th century began to take control of the Moorish Empire, covering parts of Asia and Africa. King Ferdinand and Queen Isabella started their crusade against the Moors[129] and Jews[130] of Spain. With the leadership a man name Apollinario,[131] who lead a band of holy warriors known as the Garduna, This band of army was of peasants, beggars and bandits. They plot murders and practice any kind of wrongdoing against the Moors and Jews. With the slaughter of innocent non-Christians of whom they called heathens. King Ferdinand summoned their leaders to meet with high officers of church and state. Now with a license to kill the church officials told them that all of their sins would be forgiven and all of their crimes would be pardoned. They were to be a secret society of murderers with the full approval of church and state. In the year of 1492[132] The Moors of Cordova were expelled and the Treaty of Cordova was put in place. Some of the Moors and Jews left from Spain, and the rest remained and converted to Christianity. From the many parts of the Moorish Empire the Moors and Jews settle; in many nations throughout Afru-ika and Europe and many Islands around the Atlantic Ocean. Now the seat of power of The Moorish Empire was in the hands

---

[129] Let us not forget that some of these Moors and Jews look like the Moorish chief on the cover of the book Moors in Spain.

[130] J.A Rogers 1967 Sex and Race Vol. I p. 91 Were the Jews originally negroes? "European painters and sculptors by their use of white models to typify Biblical characters have falsified tremendously the physiognomy of the ancient Jews." Gerald Massey goes on to say from the relics discovered in Africa the Jews originated in Africa. Of whom they lived for more than four centuries among the Negroid Egyptians. note: (the word negro which means black in Spanish was first used by the Europeans to describe the Moors, thus stating in all of their literature that we were black, negro and colored. Which has no connection with civilization). Our own historian and men of letters also use these terms as well for only as reference or simply they do not know or understand. It was only until Ali had let it be known about our Moorish heritage.

[131] Apollinario, who live as a hermit in the hills of Cordova, the last stronghold of the Moorish Empire, He had a vision that the Virgin Mary appointed him to be the savior of Spain and drive the Moors out of the land. He believed that he was licensed by God and the Holy Virgin to destroy the invading heathens by any means.

[132] This is very interesting that in 1492 the same date that Christopher Columbus sailed what is called America (The New World).

of the Ottoman Turks[133] and then the Moors of Morocco under the leadership of King Mohammed Ibn Abdullah.[134] By the 1670, the church and state withdrew its support from the Garduna, by now the holy warriors became a secret cult within the church and continued their attacks against all those opposed the teachings of Christianity, they expand their power to include Christians as victims to their plans. They began selling their services of murder, kidnapping and robbery. At the height of its power, the Garduna instituted ranks[135] within the society. One who was at the head was the grand master[136] next was the leader of the individual bands called chief. Then the planning of its criminal operations was called the swordsmen. The true fighting men of the society were called the athletes, tough and ruthless individuals who were often escaped convicts, galley-slaves and vicious criminals.[137] Next in rank were the bellows elderly men

---

[133] HK of the M. H. T of S. 1927 Chap. 45-V7 "The Turks are the true descendants of Hager, who are the chief protectors of the Islamic Creed of Mecca. Beginning from Mohammed the First, the founder of the uniting of Islam, by the command of the great universal God-ALLAH."

[134] Morocco became the first country in the world in 1777 to recognize U.S. independence. And granted free rights of passage to all America ships. In 1787 it became the Treaty of Peace and Friendship signed between the United States and Morocco. The signatures of Abdel-Khak, Mohammed Ibn Abuallh and George Washington. America was once apart of the Moorish Empire now America is in the hands of the European nations. (The planners of the New World).

[135] This made the ground base of organized crime in Rome Italy. The high Mafia Dons are Roman Catholic (See the movie The God Father) and they are all subordinate to the Pope of the Vatican.

[136] Evidently the connection of grand master and many of its off shoot thereof , took its origin of the Moorish Egyptian teachings of some degrees that were left in Spain and transform them into the lower sciences of Lucifer to rule and control Spain. In later years this plan expand to take control of many lands. They became fraternal guilds of Europe and called it "freeman of the craft" later they developed into the lodges of the 1700's. Now known as Masonic Lodges .

[137] In later years Europe had empty its prisoners into the new world to fight and take control of the land from the Moors (who they called Indians). The first settlers of Virginia and the leaders of the revolution had once been prisoners, criminal, debtors, political dissidents, prisoners of war, murderers, robbers and harlots. And from their descendents of hatred and violence the South became raciest of all of the colonies which produced the Ku Klux Klan (Knights of Columbus Klan) (Afrikan people and European Holidays: A Mental Genocide) 1979 Book I by Ishakamusa Barashago

who disposed of stolen goods. And the lowest rank in the Garduna was held by the goats.[138] The new recruits who had to prove their abilities. Ali was never a Shriner,[139] (A Shriner is the keeper of the dead[140]) Those who are dead were the ones who have no knowledge about their true identity.[141] Prophet Noble Drew Ali exposed the secrets of these Masons an others. The truth was hidden and falsehood was made to appear to be the true. When in the midst of security, their disguise is stripped off. And the children of Wisdom shall mock of their cunning. It was those who was trying to change the Prophet's Movement into their own order. By using those that were placed in the movement by the government. Ali's Moorish Movement is to uplift our minds nationally first. He challenged this government and our own people to recognize[142] our divine rights. Proclaiming to

---

[138] The Goat is now one of the symbols of Lucifer worshipers. The young represents their minds were easy to control and influence. Another symbol is an owl. Which is located on the front upper right hand corner dollar bill detailed frame with the number 1in it in the top left hand corner of that frame is the owl.

[139] The Shriners was founded in 1872 in New York City. by a physician and actor, there were no names given here. I wonder why?

[140] The dead were deaf, blind and dumb of not knowing who they are. They were marked with the names of negro, black, colored and African American.

[141] David Miller On Nationaity 1995 National Identity "all sub-communities in America have found adopting an American national identity as comparatively straightforward as have the immigrant Irish and Italians. American Indians have typically had a sense of their identity and a desire for political autonomy that sets them at odds with the larger community. In case of blacks, the problem is not so much one of a com-peting national identity as a difficulty in wholeheartedly adopting a national identity whose principles-equal rights, equality of opportunity-have been flouted in their own case." With that said we must look into Noble Drew Ali's statement where he said: "Those who fail to recongnize the free national name (Moorish American) of their constitutional government are classed as undesirables" So those who called themselves Black people felt that they did not need an National Identity, all they wanted was equal rights. Remember this! " In the deliberation of nations no consideration is given to a people who are not of a Nation."

[142] Moorish Literature are Excerpts taken from the Moorish Guide 1927-1928 A Divine Warning By The Prophet For The Nations "The citizens of all free national government according to their national constitution are all one family bearing one free national name. Those who fail to recognize the free national name of their constitutional government are classed as undesirables, and are subject to all inferior name and abuses and mistreatments that the citizens care to bestow upon them." This mistreatment took place under the Jim Crow laws and our ways of thinking and acting by denying the truth .

be Moorish beyond North America. **"Seamos Moros"** Let us be Moors we Cubans, wrote the Cuban[143] poet and nationalist Jose Marti in 1893. The Sir Lankan Moors trace their ancestry to Moorish traders who settled in Sri Lanka some between the eighth and fifteenth centuries.

The Indian Moors[144] are Muslims who can trace their origins to immigrants searching for business opportunities during the colonial period. Others arrived during the British period from various parts of India. During 18th and 19th centuries, Javanese and Malaysian arrived and the 19th and 20th centuries Pakistani and Indian Muslims. Ali said: From his Divine Origin of The Asiatic Nations:

> **"The Asiatic nations and countries in North, South and central America; the Moorish Americans and Mexicans in in North America, Brazilians, Argentineans and Chileans in South America. Columbians, Nicaraguans and natives of San Salvador in Central America, etc. All of these are Moslems."**[145]

---

[143] Jose Marti (1853-1895). A Cuban by the name of Brother Bartholomew Bey, in the early sixties introduced Prophet Noble Drew Ali teachings to my Uncle and from there to my father. The indigenous people in Cuba were Guanajatabey, take notice of the name Bey at the end of this name.

[144] Notice Indian Moors, this name was also used in America. They called us Indians because they were one and the same. Ali said: "The Hindoos of India, the descendants of the ancient Canaanites, Hittites and Moabites from the land of Canaan." HK of the M. H. T of S. 1927 Chap. 45-V4.

[145] HK of the M.H.T of S. 1927 Chap. 45- V5 & V6 Ali explains here that all of these countries had been converted to the rulers religion during several periods of time. Thus stating that we are the majority and not the minority and we all have the same origin as the people of Asia because the land at one time was Asia which means in Sanskrit Ushas signifying "Land of Dawn" We were known as Asiatics pertaining to Asia. When race was replaced by Nationality and Europe began to use White for themselves and give us the term Negroid. Ali explains the science of it .He said: "White means purity, purity means God, and God means ruler of the land." 1790 Congress declares the United States a white nation, and 1791 the VA legislature made the term "white" a legal distinction. Making the term "white" meaning to have access to certain forms preferential treatment, exemption from oppression, solely on the basis of European ancestry (allegedly) "white" skin. Thus, the concepts of "white people" and white privilege" share the same historical and institutional roots. (Listen to Neely Fuller Jr. on You Tube on white supremacy). There is only one race, the human race. And to be diplomatic about the two when it comes to race it will be Asiatic and European.

19th century Moorish family

In view of Latin American and Spanish history. Their culture Ancestry can be trace to northern Afru- ika. Most of the people who came to Latin America and the Spanish Caribbean were from southern Spain, Andalusia. They were Moriscos, Moors forcibly converted to Christianity. They were stripped of their religion and culture, brought to the so-called New World where they were enslaved with Afru -ikan slaves. The poet[146] Manuel Machado proudly declared himself a member of the "Moorish race, a race of the sun."[147] I was traveling on a train journeying my way from Newark

---

[146] You may notice by now that many poets of whom were proclaiming to be Moorish. This is because poets were the voices for the people and their words were an open book to the public, when at a time that people could not read they listen to the ones who express their emotions politically and socially.

[147] Google Latin Muslim history, also take note in Nature Knows no color-Line- page 68

NJ. to Richmond VA. When I arrived there, I was waiting for my ride. and as I stood there wearing a shirt that read what is your nationality? on the front, and on the back it read my nationality is Moorish American. A few steps away there was a brother standing there for about 15 minutes, suddenly he approach me and ask if I was a Moor, my reply was "yes, are you"? He said: "**I am, do you have a nationality card?**" I said: **"yours for mine."** Then we began to exchange cards and I notice on his card that read the **Moorish Holy Temple of Sciences** was from Mexico. I said praise ALLAH! I knew at this time without doubt that Ali had spent some time there also. The brother said it was no longer there but he still kept his card. I was told that Ali had said at the time that his health was getting worse that he was going to Mexico to rest his form so that he was able to come back to America to resume his mission. However that never took place. What we should know by Ali's words that our dominion and inhabitation extended from North-East and South -West Afru-ika, across the great Atlantis even unto the present North, South and Central America and also Mexico and the Atlantis Islands;[148] before the great earthquake, which cause the great Atlantic Ocean.[149] There is a lot of history concerning Mexico so let us take a look into the pages of **"African Presence In Early America"**1992 edited by Ivan Van Sertima. Nicholas, Leon, an eminent Mexican authority, reports on the oral traditions of his people.

"**The oldest inhabitants of Mexico were blacks.**" He goes on to say:

"**The existence of blacks and giants is commonly believed by**

---

offspring of these Moors and West Africans were among the discoveries of the New World and the first builders of Latin America. Sun - The realm of consciousness that has been illumined by Spirit.

[148] What is left from the Atlantis Islands from the great earthquake are the Caribbean island such as Aruba, Bahamas, Barbados, Bermuda, Cuba, Dominican Republic, Guyana, Haiti, Jamaica, Puerto Rico, Trinidad & Tobago just to name a few. Total of the thirty-three.

[149] HK of the M. H. T of S. 1927 Chap. 47 Egypt, The Capital Empire of The Dominion of Africa

nearly all races of our soil and in their various languages they had words to designate them."

Ali said that we were already here[150] as free men and women. There have been so much evidence over the years to support Ali's clam. The question here is, how or why we have not herd of them? For one thing, some of us do not like to read and there are those who do read but read the wrong books. Then there are the mis- conception of our history that was manufactured by us who were mis-educated[151] by the early European so-call historians. Ali was simply saying that some of us were enslaved here and ship to different parts of the slave trade Countries. Here is a documented statement about George Washington himself who wanted to purchase a hogshead of molasses and one of rum, two small pots of sweetmeats for sale of Tom, George's slave. Tom was the property a slave under the term negro Why do you think that they called it a slave trade?

---

[150] To support Ali's truth, you will have to read "African Presence in Early America" p. 79 Everywhere, from one corner of the ancient America world to the other, blacks were found. Not only were they here long Before Columbus, but they were here, not as slaves, but as free men, even as priest kings among the Olmecs. As R.A. Jairazbhoy has pointed out, from his book Ancient Egyptians and Chinese in America 1974. "The black began his career in America not as slave but as Master."

[151] "We are dealing here, then, mainly with information obtained from the study of negroes who have beenprofessionally trained by white in their own schools and in mixed institutions." page 74, The Mis-education Of The Negro. By Carter G. Woodson 1933.

The Prophet went to México May 21, 1928 and return June 8th 1928
Sombrero (Spanish for hat) in English refers to a type of wide-brimmed hat in Mexico. Sombreros can reflect social and economic status of a wearer.

You may notice that our Moorish history has been hidden from us for many years. right after physical slavery, the new deal was set up and put in place. It was called the reconstruction period. It was during this period that the oppressors were enforcing the negro laws upon the people. They knew in the later years to come that they will have to educate[152] them. By this time only a few could read, but many could not understand what they read. That is why we have to be told by the main stream media.[153] If they have not said that, it was true then it wasn't. This is the result of when the real truth is presented other than this main stream media or some of our

---

[152] "The main chief difficulty with the education of the negro is that it has been largely imitation resulting in the enslavement of his mind" p. 134 The Mis-education Of The Negro. By Carter G. Woodson. 1933

[153] During that time it was the Church ministers, priest and teachers. Today our so-called black people, even though we can read . It is your local news papers and nation wide cable news such as (Fox, CNN, BBC etc…). What you don't know is that they are programmed from the same oppressors, in which they are programming our minds with more false rather than the truth.

men and women of high status of degrees. We will deny it without given a single thought that this maybe true or false. By 1913 the condition[154] of the minds of the so-called negroes were at a delusion, Ali was making his way for the recovery of the minds of the people. That is why it was so important to search and to discover our Moorish history. Egyptian scripts also seem to have turned up in ancient America.[155] Have you ever heard of the archaeological cover up by the Smithsonian Institution?[156] There was a discovery at the Grand Canyon[157] of ancient artifacts, hieroglyphs, armor, statues and mummies. The area around ninety-four mile Creek and Trinity Creek had areas with the names like Tower of Set, Tower of Ra, Horus Temple, Osiris Temple, and Isis Temple. (these names were on a rock formation) There were also names such as the Cheops Pyramid, the Buddha Cloister, Buddha Temple, Manu Temple and Shiva Temple.[158] One must bare in mind that there are discovers that suppose to be hidden from us, but however the absolute truth will prevail. Have you ever took notice to the names that were placed here in North America of Arabic origin? Like the Arabic word Al as of "The" Alabama[159] derives from Ali Baba, and the capital city of Florida which is Tallahassee which means "That He

---

[154] Moorish Literature are Excerpts taken from the Moorish Guide 1927-1928 p. 8 The Voice of the Prophet " I, the Prophet, sent to redeem this nation from mental slavery which you have now, need every one of you who think that your condition can be better. This is a field open to strong men and women to uplift the nation and take your place in the affairs of men."

[155] This was said by Dr. Barry Fell (Harvard University) Saga of America 1980 The descendants of the Muslim visitors of North America are members of the present Iroquois, Algonquin, Anasazi, Hohokam and Olmec native people.

[156] This was started by a British millionaire James Smithson 1829.

[157] This story was first printed on April 5, 1909 in the Phoenix Gazette. Also watch You Tube Coast to Coast Am Archaeological cover ups by David Hatcher Childress, Egyptian caves-Grand Cayon.

[158] Within this entire area of with these names it became a forbidden a zone, because of its dangerous caves. This expedition was led by a Professor S.A. Jordan of Smithsonian. The Smithsonian claims to have no knowledge of any discovery of Egyptian and Hindu hieroglyphs etc. The map of Mexico 1821-1840 you will see that land of Mexico covered Arizona, California, Colorado, Nevada, Texas and Utah.

[159] Alabama (ALLAH bamya).

ALLAH will deliver you sometime in the future." Or Sharif for Sheriff. The ancient Cherokee identified themselves as Ani'Yun-wiya, meaning "real or principal people." Sequoyah, the Cherokee leader of the 19th Century, is best known for inventing Cherokee Syllabary[160] in 1821. There is also some tribes that reveal names from Islamic roots, Anasazi, Apache, Arawak, Arikana, Chavin Cherokee, Cree, Hohokam, Hupa, Hopi, Makkah, Mahigan, Mohawk, Nazca, Zuna, etc. The last Cherokee chief who had a Muslim name was Ramadhan Ibn Wati of the Cherokees in 1866. Did you know? that Queen Elizabeth II joined a group of the so-called American Indians[161] to pay tribute Sachem Mohamet Weyonomon, a Mohegan Indian chieftain, who died in England of smallpox in 1763. Sachem Mohamet and delegation traveled from the colony of Connecticut[162] to petition King George II for the return of Mohegan land that had been appropriated by British settlers.[163] There are many questions[164] and yet few answers from the past history of our forefathers until Noble Drew Ali brought our Illustrious history through his eyes and his experience. And In time the truth will be reveal to those who seek it. It will be the knowledge of the Moorish history and the so called-American Indian that we will get a greater understanding of our true history here in America. Moor[165] does not mean black as some

---

[160] Sequoyah's system is similar to that used in teaching Arabic language.

[161] One must remember that the true Indians comes from India. And Indi was an ancient Latin word for the so-called black people in general. The origin of Indians in America were the descendants of the Olmec and the Moguls.

[162] The " Moor's Indian Charity School" of Connecticut was founded by Reverend Eleazer Wheelock, Its main contributor was Joshua Moor, in which the school was named after. Who donated money and a house in the year of 1763. Members included Iroqouis, Delaware, Narragansetts, Mohawks, and Mohegan's. Page 39 Othello's Children In The "New World" Moorish history & Identity in the American African Experience by Jose V. Pimienta-Bey, Ph.D.

[163] BBC News Report November 22, 2006.

[164] HK of the M. H. T of S. 1927 Chap. 48-V5 That the world may hear and know the truth, that among the descendants of Africa there is still much wisdom to be learned in these days for the redemption of the sons of men under Love, Truth, Peace , Freedom and Justice.

[165] Moor 1913 Webster 1.One of a mixed race inhabiting Morocco, Algeria, Tunis, and Tripoli, mainly along the coast and in towns. 2. (Hist.) Any individual of the swarthy races

will say. Claud Anderson, ED. D. in his book Black Labor White Wealth said: **"Since color was the decisive factor in slavery, it was important to know who was and was not a member of the black race. Moors were not classified as members of the black race."**[166]

Remember now, black is an adjective not a race or your nationality,[167] in which that means there is a relationship between a person and their state of origin, culture, association, affiliation and/or loyalty. To give more enlightenment on this subject we must review J.A. Rogers book **Nature Knows No Color-Line** on page 72 where he said in his research that Sir William Smith said:

> **"Moors were known in Alexandrian dialect as "Blacks," and that "the Moors....must not be considered a different race from the Numidians."**[168]

You see when the Europeans[169] were writing they saw us as black people and negroes regardless what we called our-selves they were the ones who defined us with these marks. And through time we took on these terms as

---

of Africa or Asia which have Adopted the Mohammedan religion. Long before the name Morocco Noble Drew Ali said that we are the descendants of the ancient Moabites who inhabited the Northwestern and Southwestern shores of Afru-ika. The modern name for the Moabites is Moroccans. Moor or Moorish consist of cultural, langrage and land.

[166] Page 110 It will continue to say that in northwest Africa, the offspring of the blacks, white Berbers and Arabs became known as Moors. One should know that the name Berbers was derived from the word Barbarian. The name Moor or Moorish was used way before the word black.

[167] Nationality - 1913 Webster's - Existence as a distinct or individual nation, national unity and integrity. Also the state or quality of belonging to or being connected with a nation or government by nativity, character, ownership and allegiance. Note* More of the word nationality in chapter III the message.

[168] Numidia (202 BC - 46 BC) was an ancient so called Berber kingdom in present -day Algeria and part of Tunisia (North Africa) Its people were the Numidians.

[169] Nature Knows No Color-Line 1952 J.A. Rogers p. 72 The word, Moor or More, signifies a primitive black population. Since, therefore, Romans invaded Britain, France, Belgium, Germany and other parts of Europe, they undoubtedly took the word "Moor," meaning a black people, with them. In fact, so common was the use of "Moor" for Negroes that it is astonishing to find some writers calling Moors, a white race.

well. Noble Drew Ali was teaching that the Moors[170] were the descendants of the ancient Moabites. He knew in time that we will develop technology in the future, he called it the electrified age.[171] During this time the truth will be known to the world, but in order to accept it, your mind must be free from those of whom corrupt our minds with falsehood. Once our minds have been free we will discover the truth all around us in this falsehood world which is full of lies. This comes to mind that we may find true answers of our history between the pages of time, but we have to look way beyond the so-called black and negroes. With in our own history we came from many civilizations so therefore we had many names[172] that formed many lands.[173] There was no black[174] land with people, Kemet (Egypt) which means "black" only designates the black soil of Egypt, rather than the black man.[175]

Moors is an Ancient[176] name we will find most of our lost history with the name Moor or Moorish. By 1927 to 1929 Noble Drew Ali found it necessary to interpret our own history, sciences, culture and religion etc. And not of the interpretations of Western thoughts that have enslaved the minds of the people. You see Noble Drew Ali knew something about the

---

[170] Ibid. p. 79 Moor goes too far back in prehistory to be relevant. When the Greeks and Romans used that word they definitely meant human beings. One thing is certain, Greeks and Latin have Egyptian linguistic influences although both are Indo-European languages. The ancient Greeks were from Africa.

[171] Television , radio, text, internet/, face book & tweeter etc. (where we can use them to gain information).

[172] HK of the M. H. T of S. 1927 Chap. 47-V6 The Moabites, Canaanite, Hittite and Amorite

[173] Ibid, p.58 according to all true and divine records of the human race there is no negro, blackcolored race attached to the human family.

[174] 100 Amazing facts About The Negro 1934 by J.A. Rogers p. 48 Black and Colored on the other hand, have no historic meaning whatever for African peoples. And The African Origin Of Civilization 1955 by Cheikh Anta Diop page 48 Scientifically speaking, there is no dark red race. The term was launched only to create confusion. There is no really black man in exact sense of the word.

[175] The African Origin Of Civilization 1955 by Cheikh Anta Diop p. 7

[176] 100 Amazing facts About The Negro by J.A. Rogers page 22 The most ancient name for the so-called black people was Moor from Ancient Egypt .

name Moor[177] that we were not taught at that time. If someone taught you something new it was very difficult to understand it, because the condition our of minds were in a state of denial, we were a people of belief.[178] If we take a look before 1492 the darker skinned tribes of North America were a result of Olmec which produce the Mexicans and out from them the Aztec, Inca, Toltec, Mixtec, and Mayans. The Mayans were the descendants of the Malian Moors also known as the Olmecs. They were referred to as the so-called "Black Mexicans" or Quetzacoatl. And from the same blood of the Olmecs, Arapaho, Arikara, Blackfoot, Cheynne, Crow, Apache, Mandan, Pawnee and the Yamasee in which came the Washitaw. The Yamasee is the mother tribe of the Creeks, Seminoles, Apaches, Choctaw, Chickasaw, Catawb and Cherokee.[179] In the year of 1790, South Carolina passed the Moors Sundry Act.[180] The Sumter country census recorded the name Joseph Benenhaly, and with that name came the black codes and laws that was used against the so-called negroes. But his real name was Yusef Ben Ali a Moslem from Morocco. with this act he regained full national status. It was said that his dark-skinned descendants were know as the Turks of Sumter County, South Carolina. The "Turks," a colony of some 300 persons, have petitioned the federal court of eastern district of South Carolina for admittance to the Hillcrest School for white children in Sumter county. In the Virginia Code[181] of 1682 states in Act I.

---

[177] The African Origin Of Civilization 1955 by Cheikh Anta Diop p. 144 Many African Moslems alter their genealogical tree, adding branches back to Mohammed, thus claiming Moroccan ancestry.

[178] HK of the M. H. T of S. 1927 Chap. 7-V 28 Belief is first, and this is what man thinks, perhaps, is truth.

[179] There were many tribe leaders Coacoochee or wild cat (Seminole) Cohia or John Horse (Seminole) Geronimo (Apache) Tecumseh and his brother Tenskwatawa (Shawnee) Tatanka Yotanka or Sitting Bull (Sioux) For more information read Black Indians a hidden heritage 1986 by William Loren Katz.

[180] This act was enacted by the legislative body to grant special status to the subjects of the Sultan of Morocco. They petitioned the legislature to rule that they were not subject to the laws that governed blacks and slaves.

[181] Black Laws of Virginia Guild 1936 - This book deals exclusively with the status of the Virginia Negro, bond and free, as traced through the laws, resolutions and ordinances of

> "It is enacted that all servants, except Turks and Moors, while in amity with his majesty which shall be imported into this country either by sea or land, whether Negroes, Moors, Mulattoes or Indians who and whose parentage and native countries are not Christian at the time of their first purchase by some Christians, although, afterward and before their importation into this country they shall be converted to the Christian faith."

When such names as Moors, Turks, Negroes, mulattoes or Indians are put in place in any documents from the government we need to know who they were at that time. Because they will change what they are in time to have you to think what they are known now. For example did you know that on May 24, 1775 and appeared in Savannah Georgia Gazette reporting runaway slaves. It read that the plantation of Lachlan M Gillivray at Vale Royal naming three Muslims: Quammie, about 30 years old; Sambo, about 22 years and a Moor; and another Sambo, about 25 years old. There are many runaways recorded between 1765 and 1776 with some ads saying yellow complexion and Moorish breed.[182] A researcher C.A. Weslager interviewed the "Indian Moors" of Delaware who were known as the Nanticoke and Moors of Delaware[183] and he asked them if they were black or white, and how do they classified themselves, they responded: "We are Moors" they also rejected the marks as being Negro, Black and Colored. It was said that they identified as both " Indians and Moors" as early as 1855.[184] You see Noble Drew Ali (the teacher) treads the way; on every

---

the Virginia Assembly. Law always reflects the social condition and thinking of the people who made it.

[182] Muslims in America 1998 Seven Centuries of History (1312-9198) by Amir Nashid Ali Muhammad

[183] The Nanticoke Indians: Past and Present 1983 by C.A Weslager and Delaware's Forgotten Folks: The story of the Moors and Nanticoke 1943 by C.A. Weslager.

[184] Othello's Children in the "New World" 2002 p. 144 by Jose Pimienta-Bey, Ph.D. He received his B. A. in history from Gettysburg College in 1984 and his M. A. in history from Shippensburg University in 1987. He earned his Ph. D. in African American Studies from Temple University in 1995.

span of ground. He leaves his footprints[185] clearly cut for those who has their eyes wide open to see and to be assured that Noble Drew Ali will show you the way. From the past pages I have mentioned about Noble Drew Ali was born from the Cherokee nation, giving us a insight with Indians and Moors being the same term during another era, of cause this will share some light from past author's who record these names in there time viewing from both sides of the Atlantic. David Mac Ritchie book **Ancient and Modern Britons Vol. I** said:

"In 1676 the natives races of New England were spoken of indiffererently as Indians and Moors; and our British Indian are also remembered as Moors."[186]

What is the meaning of Noble Drew Ali when he said that we are Moorish Americans[187] The Moors are the descendants of the ancient Moabites who inhabited many parts of North, South and Central American before The European invasion[188] of many lands in Africa and Europe. The

---

[185] The Science of the word (footprints) was a lesson for us to look for important information hidden within (foot notes) that where printed in many books covering many subjects.

[186] Ancient and Modern Britons Vol. I 1884 by David Macritchie p. 374 and 375 take notice from the same book p. 277 In short, these turf-built wigwams (tepees) are the dwellings of the Scoto-Picts, or Egyptian Moors, whether we look at these people in their latest individual form, or at an earlier date than that-when they formed an important political entity in the British Island (which their civilized and hybrid descendants still do) And their dwellings form one of the very numerous links that unite the painted "Moors" of Scotland with certain kindred races in Europe, Asia ,and America.

[187] Noah Webster Dictionary 1828 American, n. A native America; originally applied to the aboriginals, or copper-colored races, found here by Europeans; but now applied to the descendants of Europeans born in America. If you will take a cooper penny and placed it on the back of your hand you will see the true cooper- colored people who were the original inhabitants of this land they called America.

[188] The legacy of fifteenth century religious prejudice - When Christopher Columbus first set foot on the sands of Guanahani island, he performed a ceremony to " take possession" of the land for the king and queen of Spain, acting under the international laws of Western Christendom. This was based on a religious now known in history as the Doctrine of Discovery. To understand the connection between Christendom's principle of discovery and the laws of the United States, we need to begin by examining a papal document issued forty years before Columbus historic voyage in 1452, Pope Nicholas

name Moor was well known in Africa in fact in his book **Stolen Legacy** by George James[189] he said:

> "In the 8th century A.D. the Moors invaded Spain and took with them, the Egyptian culture which they had preserved." (page 39) "The Moors were recognized custodians of African culture, to whom the world looked for enlightenment." (page 40) In Nature knows No Color Line Moor was another name for Ethiop (page 49) and Moor was once a symbol of power in all of Europe at a time prowess in battle ranked first, the Moors had a reputation second to none. (page 99)

most Afru-ikans were called Moors so during the slave trade from Medieval Afru-ikans to American we were actually Moors. Moorish (Moors) was the last name we were under before we were put into slavery. If you will research the name Moor or Moorish throughout history you will see these names is almost everywhere such as in the book **Golden Age Of The Moors**[190] history of the Moors in Africa and Europe it was

---

directed King Alfonso to capture, vanquish, and subdue the Saracen, (Moors) pagans, and enemies of Christ, to put them into perpetual slavery, and take all their possession and property. The lesson to be learned is that the papal bulls of 1452 and 1493 issued by Pope Alexander VI on May 4, are but two clear examples of how the "Christian Powers," were authorized to conqueror in America to justify an incredibly brutal system of colonization which dehumanized the indigenous people by regarding their territories as being inhabited by brute animals in other words the Christian "Law of Nations" asserted that Christian nations had the divine right, based on the Bible, to claim absolute title to and ultimate authority over any newly "discovered" Non-Christian inhabitants and their lands. This belief gave rise to the Doctrine of Discovery used by Spain, Portugal, England, France, Holland and all Christian nations.

[189] Dr. James Granville Monah James was born in Georgetown, Guyana, South America. He earned his Bachelor of Arts, Bachelor of Theology and Master of Arts from Durham University in England. He con-ducted research at London University and did postgraduate work at Columbia University where he read for his Ph. D James earned a teaching certificate in the State of N.Y. to teach mathematics, Latin and Greek. Dr. James's tragic death, under mysterious circumstances, reputedly, came shortly after his 1954 Stolen Legacy's publication.

[190] Golden Age of The Moor 1992 edited by Ivan Van Sertima who was born in Guyana, South America. He was educated at the school of Oriental and African Studies, London

written that Catholics was very much aware of the superior knowledge of the Moors and they made efforts to acquire that knowledge so that they would not be left too far behind. In relation to Moorish Science and knowledge nearly all the major universities in Europe was influence by Moorish mathematics[191], chemistry,[192] medicine[193], astronomy, music, science, navigation, architecture, and food. For the Moorish culture and learning some Europeans respect and or envy Moorish Sciences and yet many Catholics resisted our Moorish knowledge in as so much that several Europeans mimicked[194] Moorish customs and manners. This is why they dress up in our Moorish Egyptian attire and adorn our Fes (Fezz) and symbols and call themselves Masons (Ma son/ Mother son) in which they used our sciences to construct the building of what they call America, (New World Order) North American was known as Egypt of the West.[195] Lets revisited **Ancient and Modern Britons Vol. I** on pages 230 & 231 it read: **"Just as Indians are permitted to leave their reservations, after receiving a "pass' from authorities. But, in the following century, owing to a**

University and Rutgers Graduate School and holds degrees in African Studies, Linguistics and Anthropology.

[191] Moors were advanced in mathematics, the solving of quadratic equations and the development of new concepts of trigonometry.

[192] Moorish chemistry refined upon gunpowder invention in China and introduced the first shooting mechanisms, know as firesticks. Known today as rifles and fire arms.

[193] Moorish advances in pathology, aetiology (study of diseases), therapeutics, surgery and pharmacology. Texts were written by Moorish physicians describing surgical technique and the instruments that were used. The Physicians were academically trained scholars and had to pass a licensing exam before beginning his practice. With a code prescribed to be understanding, unselfish, kindness and discretion they also must always keep their body clean. Their dress code was to ware white attire. All of this and more in medieval in Moorish Andalusia.

[194] Moorish Literature are Excerpts taken from the Moorish Guide 1927-1928 p. 20 "other groups of people in the city have been using the dress of our forefathers and imitating them all but the olive hue they cannot get.

[195] Actually in the Moorish teachings of Noble Drew Ali from the Mason Dixon line on down is Egyptian land. The Mississippi river was known as the River Nile which ends in southern Illinois, near a city with an Egyptian name – Cairo. In which the river meets the Ohio river. The Mounds in Cahokia are the biggest pyramids in North America. Serach for the mound builders.

temporary dominance of the intolerant and merciless Spirit that is yet displayed by the white rowdies of the fast-vanishing "frontier" in the United States, those Moors that still infested the borders were subjected, as we have seen, to a more despotic treatment."

In 1516 a map of Florida, based on a French expedition, shows three names that may indicate an early Moorish settlement there.[196] During my early days in school back in the sixties we were not taught about the truth of America and our people. I loved history but I have always felt that we were being brain washed with his story of lies. What is really disturbing is that some of us believed it, even unto this day. Just take a look at the 4th of July,[197] we celebrate proudly, as if we have our own independence. Have you ever thought that in 1776 our people were beaten, abused, murdered, sold as cattle and our women being raped and this was all in the name of slavery,[198] what was our people thinking about! Did you know that it was practice and established in the Spanish colonies as early as 1560. By now you should know that the Moors were in Spain and they were expelled in 1492 or convert to Christianity. For those that were expelled, where did you think they went to? Ah, it was in England before Great Britain prohibited it subjects from participating in the slave trade,[199] 600,000 and 650,000? Afru-ikan (Moors) had been forcibly trans- ported to North America. It was said that the face of slavery began to change from the

---

[196] African Presence in Early America p. 133 edited by Ivan Van Sertima

[197] Please read Frederick Douglass speech "The meaning of July Fourth for the Negro" (July 5, 1852)

[198] Slave labor existed as a legal institution from the English Colony in Virginia 1619.

[199] It may be some of interest to watch a film called "Amazing Grace" based on a true story about a man name William Wilberforce who's quest to the end the British slave trade.

"tawny[200]"Indian[201] to the "black moor"[202] Afru-ika in the years between 1650 and 1750. This was said because those names will cover here in America and Afru-ika etc. The more you research on the name Moor you will have to take notice and ask these Questions of who, what, where, why and how? The reason is simple, it is because without these questions how could you enlightened your mind with a certain knowledge of truth on the subject in which you have studied. Who was here in Ancient America? Lets revisited Ivan Van Sertima's book[203] once again. He said: **"Ferdinand Columbus describes the Indian cotton garments as "breechcloths of the same design describes and cloth as shawls worn by the Moorish women of Grenada." Cortes' Report on the dressing habits of the Indians of Mexico is more detailed. He remarked that "The clothing which they wear is like long veils, the men wear breechcloths about their bodies, and large mantles, very thin, and painted in the style of Moorish draperies"[204]**

When you study the true history of the Roman Christians you will find that they were destroying the books to erase our illustrious history.[205]

---

[200] Tawny, which they say it means orangey brown tinged with gold.

[201] Indian is relating to India or its people and those in America as they were called Indians because Columbus thought he was in India which we know now why they were called Indians (Moors) In the early years of the 18th century, the number of Native American (Indian) slaves in areas such as Carolinas may have been as much as half of the African slave population.

[202] Blackamoor which was said to be a taboo term for black person or somebody with very dark skin.

[203] African Presence in Early America p. 201 and 202.

[204] Ibid p. 202 he continue and said: "The Moorish elements described in these accounts could just as well apply to the Muslim Mandinga who at that time exhibited many of the same dress styles.

[205] Moorish Literature are Excerpts taken from the Moorish Guide 1927-1928 p. 11 A Historical Letter From Prophet Noble Drew Ali Reincarnated (Brother John Givens EL). The Europeans took the birthright away from the people whom they forced under bondage. They were not slaves, they were bound free men.The subsequent generation who followed them in bondage were slaves because their minds had been subjugated to a European psychology. They were separated from the illustrious history of their forefatherswho were the founders of civilization.

So when we were taught that Christopher Columbus discovered America, perhaps most of the people will believe it with out any questions. Prophet Noble Drew Ali's teachings gave a shock to the American people, they did not know what to think. But for some, he has open their eyes to the truth about the history of America, Jesus, Islam, and being the descendant of the ancient Moabites. The most controversy is that America is Africa, you see the Europeans has flip the maps and change some of the original names and dates of places that were placed by our ancient forefathers. Of course this must sound aspersed, However lets really look into The Moorish Holy Koran chapter 47

Egypt, The Capital Empire of The Dominion of Africa

"The Moabites from the land of Moab who received permission from the PHARAOHS of Egypt to settle and inhabit North-West Africa; they were the founders and are the true possessors of the present Moroccan Empire. With their Canaanite, Hittite and Amorite brethren who sojourned from the land of Canaan seeking new homes. Their dominion and inhabitation extended from North-East and South-West Africa, across the great Atlantis even unto the present North, South and Central America and also Mexico and the Atlantis Islands; before the great earthquake, which caused the great Atlantic Ocean."

At this time I will give you some important information from some historians that will share some light of the truth of what Noble Drew Ali was sharing with us from his chapter Egypt, The Capital[206] Empire[207] of The Dominion[208] of Africa. The key names that you will find is Egypt,

---

[206] Capital- Geography politics seat of government: a city that is the seat of government of a country, state, or province.

[207] Empire- land ruled by single authority: a group of nations, territories.

[208] Dominion- land ruled: The land governed by ruler. Or self -governing part of the Empire.

Africa, Mexico, and America. Now remember, before the great earthquake (The flood as mentioned in our Holy Bible). There were the continent of Mu known as Lemuia located in the pacific ocean and the continent of Atlantis which was located in the Atlantic ocean. They were people living at both locations which migrated in different parts of the land including American. These people today will be known as the so-called black people. With Noble Drew Ali's teachings of the genealogy of Cush[209] and his father Ham[210] you will see the many family branches of our people that became the Divine Origin of the Asiatic Nations.[211] Now before the coming of Columbus in America, the inhabitants in North America were already mix, that is why there were so many tribes of nations of whom they were called native Americans. It was said that numerous evidence suggest that Muslims (Moors) from Spain and West Africa arrived in Americas at least five centuries before Columbus. The year China discovered America[212] Cheng He arrived before Columbus by 71 years. A Chinese historical document known as the Sung document records the voyage of Muslim sailors to a land called as Mu-Lan-Pi (America) 1178. This may come as a connection but there was a thesis by Harold Sterling Gladwin[213] in his authorship of a controversial 1947 publication entitled **Men Out of Asia.** That his studies backed by specialized field research that claims that the earliest American population were the so-called Black people. With that in mind you must read **African Presence in Early Asia.**[214] Thus it said:

---

[209] Cush or Kush was Noah's grandson they became the Nubian and Abyssinian (Ethiopian) people.

[210] Ham or Cham was the son of Noah his name can also be spelled Khem for the land Kemet (Egypt) his other children were Phut, Mizraim offspring.

[211] HK of the M. H. T. of S 1927 Chap. 45 The Divine Origin of The Asiatic Nations

[212] In 1421, Cheng He- The legendary Chinese admiral: Cheng He (A Muslim) traveled around the world in the fifteenth century. British marine historian Gavin Manzies proves in his book 1421 " The year China discovered America" This document was mentioned in another publication (the Khotan Amiers) published in 1933 after Cheng He voyages.

[213] Harold Sterling Gladwin 1883-1983 was a early 20th century archaeologist that specialized in south -western archaeology of the United States. He was also known for his famed excavations at Snaketown, Arizona.

[214] African Presence in Early Asia 1985 Edited by Runoko Rashidi co-edited by Ivan Van

"We now know, based on recent scientific studies of DNA, that modern humanity originated in Africa,[215] that African people are the world's original people. Since the first modern humans (Homo sapiens[216]) in Asia were of African birth, the land mass within the span of modern humanity. But not only were African people the first inhabitants of Asia."[217]

Look into Prophet Noble Drew Ali 's Koran Questions for The Moorish Americans.

Q57. Who were Adam and Eve? They are the Mothers and Fathers of the Human family, Asiastics and Moslems.

Q58. Where did they go? They went into Asia.

Q59. What is the modern name given to their children? Asiatics.

Adam were the tribe of males and Eve was the tribe of Females.

Sertima. Runoko Rashidi is a historian, research specialist, writer, world traveler, and public lecturer focusing on the African presence globally and the African foundations of the world civilizations. He is particularly drawn to the African presence in Asia, Australia, and Pacific Islands. If you Google image on Orientalist Art you will find Moorish images. (so -call black men and women with and without their Fez and Turbans)

[215] HK of the M. H. T. of S 1927 Chap. 47- V9 "According to all true and divine records of the human race there is no negro, black, or colored race attached to the human family, because all the inhabitants of Africa were and are of the human race."

[216] Noble Drew Ali does not support that the bipedal ape evolved to man. According to the teaching's from the Moorish Holy Koran chap. 11 "Jesus and Barata-Together They Read The Sacred Books" Barata was told that man had evolved from beast or bird until it has reached the form of man. Jesus had enlightened Barata Arabo and said this: "Do you remember, Arabo, when you were ape, or bird or worm? Now, if you have no better proving of your plea than that the priest have told you so, you do not know; you simply guess." Homo Sapien in Latin means wise man or intelligent and knowing man. You will have to study the ancient history of Asia, Africa and America's people at that time to see from the different Ages of what was created for the advancement of our civilization.

[217] There is abundant evidence to show that the so-called black people within documented historical periods created or influenced some of ancient Asia's most important and enduring high-cultures.

Becoming the Fathers and Mothers[218] of civilization. They are Asiatics which were the Divine origin of the Asiatic nations, their family[219] branches of children extended to all of the seven true continents. Some have kept their covenant with their Universal Creator by living in peace as a Moslem (Peace) and there were those of whom have not kept their covenant. So to say they have been good and bad in all people throughout our illustrious ancient history. Now our oldest and ancient language teaches us that Asia in Sanskrit (Ushas) means signifying "Land of Dawn" Our Sciences shows us in its metaphysical meaning as "rise, dawn, beginning." Therefore, Asia must signify the inner, spiritual, individual consciousness (where in lay the beginning of man's conscious existence, where in lies the dawn) or rise of the light and wisdom of his/her new spiritual understanding and realization. Now back to **African Presence in Early Asia,** it was referencing all of the Afru-ikans populations that have peopled Asia[220] within both the prehistoric and historic periods. This includes Afru-ikan people as the first modern humans in Asia. The subsequent migrations and movements of Afru-ikan people impacting the essential character and content of classical

---

[218] Holy Quran by Maulana Muhammad Ali 7th edition Chap. 16 V72 "And Allah has made wives for you from among yourselves, and has given you sons and daughters from your wives, and has provided you with good things." HK of the M. H. T. of S 1927 Chap. 44 Misery V7 "There is but one way for man to be produced; there are a thousand by which he may be destroyed."

[219] Human family - Those who descend from one common progenitor; a tribe, clan, or kindred; house; as the human family. (People who have Melanin).

[220] African Presence in Early Asia 1985 p.16 we enter early China with the black dwarfs. The First Chinese emperor, Fu-His (2953-2838 B.C.) who is a wooly-haired negro. His achievements (creation of government, social institutions like marriage, writing) What is particularly interesting is that the Shang dynasty (1766-1100 B.C.) was largely a black dynasty and that the Shang were given the name of Nakhi (Na-black, khiman) by the Moso, because of their very complexion. The Cho who conquered the Shang described the inhabitants of the area as having black skin. Krishna (1200 B.C.) and Guatama Buddha (600 B.C.) of India and Jesus (100 B.C. or 33 A.D ?). The parallels between Krishna, the Black Christ of India, and the Jesus of the Gospels, are so remarkable that the latter almost seems to be a reincarnation of the former. Buddha who is represented as a man with wooly hair and Africoid features. Jesus, himself was appear in his first physical representation as a man with wooly hair. Holy Bible Rev. Chap. 1-V14 " His head and his hairs were white like wool."

Asian civilizations. A German art historian and collector Alexander Von Wuthenau said in his 1975, book,

Unexpected Faces in Ancient America.

"Von Wuthenau specifically identifies a group of carved heads as "Moorish-looking." Found within Mexico, such heads are dated between 300 - 900 C.E and another between 900 - 1500 C.E. (common era) One artifact was a old man with a hat, clearly resembles that of an old man wearing a Fez" In his book on describing the Olmec[221] Heads on pages 64 and 65 he said this: **"Twelve colossal Olmec heads from Mexico ethnically analyzed. Upper row: predominantly Negroid. Lower row: predominantly Asiatic"**

What I have witnessed was, you can not tell them apart from one or the other. They were both found in Mexico and made by the same people. Therefore they are the same. By now you should know that there is no race called Negroid, in which was described by European writers. But he was correct by saying Asiatic. Dr. Barry Fell a New Zealand archaeologist and linguist of Harvard University introduced in his book **Saga America** 1980. With his solid scientific evidence supporting the arrival, centuries before Columbus, of Muslims from North and West Africa. Dr. Fell discovered the existence of Muslim Schools in Nevada, Colorado, New Mexico, and Indiana dating back to 700-800 C.E. The language of the Pima people in the South West and the Algonquian language had many words in their vocabulary that were Arabic in origin, and Islamic rock carving were found in places like Inyo county, California. Which stated in Arabic "Yasus ben Maris" (Jesus, son of Mary") The descendants of Muslim of North America are members of the present Iroquois, Algonquin, Anasazi, Hohokam and Olmec people. American historian and linguist Leo Weiner also of Harvard University, in his book Africa and **The Discovery of America**

---

[221] The Olmecs heads were found in Vera Cruz Mexico in 1939 by Dr. Matthew Sterling. The Olmecs date back to the archaic period and the Olmec civilization parallels the dynastic periods of Egypt. It also points evidence that the Olmecs being of African ancestry.

1920 wrote that Columbus was well aware of the Mandinka presence in the New World and that the West African Muslims had spread throughout the Caribbean, Central, South and North American territories, including Canada. The West African Muslims were the Moors of Morocco with such names as "Marabitine" and "Marabios' which was related to "Marabout" (Murabit): the "Holy Men and Women" of the Moorish Empire. The Marabouts were the protectors of African Muslim frontiers, in which Van Sertima reveals. The famed Ibn Battuta[222] spoke of the Marabouts in his renowned " travels." The antiquity of such a " Moorish" (Afru-ikan) presence in the Americas is hereby seen to be quite early when one considers the significance of all the evidence presented here. Noble Drew Ali's words from his **Moorish Holy Koran** in reference with truth.[223] Lamaas ask his friend Jesus:

> **"Of understanding, what have you to say?" And Jesus said: "It is the rock on which man builds himself; it is the gnosis[224] of the aught and of the naught, of falsehood and of truth."**

Now truth is but one and it comes in many different directions to get to the understanding of the oneness of the truth, just like in a puzzle which have so many pieces to make up the whole picture. That is why there were so many books that I have suggested for reader to read, so that you may see for yourself the truth that it bares and understand the propaganda of falsehood. That is why we need to learn both because man is truth and

---

[222] Abu Abdullah Muhammad Ibn Battuta born in Tangier Morocco February 25,1304 - 1368 or 1369 He is considered one of the greatest travelers of all time. This Moorish traveler that span thirty years which extended beyond North Africa, The Horn Africa, West Africa, Southern Europe and Eastern Europe to the Middle East, South Asia, Central Asia, Southeast Asia and China surpassing Marco Polo. For more reading look into Native American Muslim, Islam in America before Columbus, Islam in Latin America and Muslim legacy in early Americas.

[223] HK of the M. H. T. of S 1927 Chap. 7 The Friendship of Jesus and Lamaas-Jesus Explains to Lamaas the Meaning of truth.

[224] Gnosis - Knowledge of Spiritual matters mystical knowledge.

falsehood strangely mixed.[225] Now the rock is symbolizing his or her faith which means the surety of the omnipotence of Allah and man.[226] rock was used as a metaphor so that I may introduce to you a book called **"When Rocks Cry Out"**[227] The Author stated this:

> "The two Atlantic Sea crossing by Mali explorers became more important when I noticed that the "Moorish." "black" Aztecs had arrived at Mexico, in ships, about the same time that Mali sent her ships across the Atlantic."

Prophet Noble Drew Ali said it best about our dominion and habitation, that our people are global and not to define us all, in one continent. Western thought teaches its people about dis-unity, you see the philosophy of this is division. It was their vision to cause disunity among many minds, such as this word they call race where as much was divided into two classes of people of whom they classified as Black /white. This was also used for the rich and the poor, Christianity and Islam, Cowboys and Redskins etc. The result of this leads to superiority, war, and competition, all motivated by fear. That's why the real truth about our history here in American was rewritten so that those early readers will carry on those lies and they will support it as well to the near future. They are known as the early historians of the colonial European societies. It is important to understand that falsehood can at times be so real that you actually think that it was the truth. Noble Drew Ali gave us something to think about. Once you have given some thought to it, in time the truth will come clear. This came clear to me from the book **"When Rocks Cry Out"**

> **"Spanish writers**[228] **who saw the Aztecs, and who knew the Moors,**

---

[225] Ibid. Chap. 7- V12 And Jesus said: "Man is truth and falsehood strangely mixed."

[226] Ibid. Chap. 7- V23 And Jesus said: "Faith is the surety of the omnipotence of Allah and man; the certainty that man will reach deific life.

[227] When Rocks Cry Out 2009 by Horace Butler #1 best seller.

[228] Ibid. p. 36 The two Atlantic Sea crossing by the Mali explorers became more important

had revealed that the Aztecs even wore the same clothing used by the Africans called Moors."

One thing that I have learned, is that the truth will come in time from those who seek it, and that truth shall set you free. The Author revealed some very interesting information, as he said:

"I had seen ancient records that unveiled the world's most explosive secret. 'Egypt' had crossed the Atlantic Sea, in ships, more than 10,000 years before the time of Christ. They built the world's largest cities, in South and Central America, and Mexico. They had united those city-states into a nation that stretched from brazil in South America to Mexico, and into Africa. I had broken the seal on 'forbidden histories.' I had found the writings that told how Egypt had built its most powerful empire, and it happened in the Americas."

This information will give some support to Noble Drew Ali's teachings from his Divine Origin Of The Asiatic Nations[229] and "Egypt, The Capital Empire Of The Dominion Of Africa."[230] But wait there is more from the Author Horace Butler, as he had express this:

"The old stones were ready to tell anyone who would listen that those Africans had built an Egypt in the Americas before they built the monument-filled in Egypt in northeast Africa. The ancient histories explained that the Africans came to Americas and built cities from Brazil to Mexico, and possibly further north."

Prophet Noble Drew Ali asked this question, What is meant by the

---

when I noticed that the "Moorish," black" Aztecs arrived at Mexico, in ships, about the same time that Mali sent her ships across the Atlantic.

[229] HK of the M. H. T. of S 1927 Chap. 45 The Divine Origin of The Asiatic Nations.
[230] Ibid. Chap. 47 Egypt, The Capital Empire of The Dominion of Africa.

word Negro[231]? Negro, a name given to a river in West Africa by the Moors, because it contains black water. What Noble Drew Ali was teaching us is to research the name Negro river and when you do you will understand that the word Negro in Spanish means black and that the location of West Afru-ika that he is referring is actually in South America, Therefore, he was redirecting our minds to our illustrious history that has been in Central and South American as well as other lands in which our ancient forefathers inhabited. Now the science of the sacred power[232] of the name Moor is hidden within its vowel[233] sounds[234] which gives a high energy, especially with two OO. If you would say Moor you can actually feel the vibration resonate in your body. The vowel O has an element of water.[235] The keynote to water is Justice/balance, the O gives power and stability and it represent faithful. The vibration of O gives the ability to attain high spiritual judgment. You see the sound of the spoken word can be measured by the rate of vibration. This means that whatever appeals to you is where your consciousness lies, and that level of consciousness is revealed by the words you speak. The study of languages[236] and its various sounds has a long and ancient[237] history. I was told that Prophet Noble Drew said: "Names have meaning" In order to wake up some of his people Prophet Noble Drew

---

[231] Koran Questions for Moorish Americans 1928 Question 86.

[232] The Sacred Power in Your Name 1998 by Ted Andrews Ted full - time author, student, and teacher in the metaphysical and spiritual fields.

[233] Ibid p. 25 The Mystical Vowels - vowels have the activating or life-giving power they are linked to archetypal elements and energies within the universe.

[234] Ibid p. 25 -vowels as "musical tones made by a regular vibration of the vocal cords and modified by varying the shape and size of the resonance chamber." Every society throughout the world has taught the power of sound and music, both as a healing force and as a force for alchemical change. Vowels are the inner power of words and it holds the strongest influence upon us. "M" is the most sacred of all letters, for it symbolizes water, where life began.

[235] Water qualities - understanding, emotional, psychic, sensitive, artistic and reserved.

[236] HK of the M. H. T. of S 1927 Chap. 35 Religion V20 "He hath fitted thee with language, to improve thy society."

[237] The power of names and spoken word was commonly recognized among the ancient traditions. The ancients also used zymology in name and languages to communicate many of their teachings.

Ali had to use Science, This was done because of the opposition will be unaware of its progress. You can judge a Prophet by his works, words and deeds. And so his sciences was his works.[238] Just as Jesus used science as well, he spoke in parables because it was a prudent teaching strategy. It was through the parables that he could enlighten those minds that were sincere and receptive. Jesus spoke of this science in Matthew 13 V9 "He who has ears to hear, let him hear" This strategy of parables will open their spiritual eyes and ears and be enlightened to the truth. So one should may think, that is the real reason behind Noble Drew Ali's statement

"If I can get you to think you can save yourself."

There is so much to cover on the name Moor we have to sum it up with the words from Jose V. Pimienta -Bey's book **Othello's Children In The New World.**

"In view of all the historical, theological & etymological evidence presented, it should be clear that the term "Moor" justifiably designates a phenotypically Africoid people with ancient origins in both Africa and near-Asia. Historical records reveal the strong ethnic ties between the "Moors" and the ancient peoples of Canaan, Moab, Phoenica, Chaldea, Kush, and Kemet. Moorish peoples are found residing in various parts of the world and not simply in the northwestern coner of African continet or in the Iberian peninsula"

The Moors, according to Oxford English Dictionary, are people who are commonly supposed to be black or very dark and it is synonymous with the word for "Negro" in many context. OED began 1857 by the philological society of London, in 1879 The society made an agreement with Oxford University Press to begin work on a New English Dictionary. Key view point is that the word supposed to be black or very dark. Take notice that during the European Renaissance, explorers, writers and scholars

---

[238] Works - The example of his life.

began to apply the term Moor to Blacks in general. Remember, that the English language are those who speak it in England, just like those who speak Spanish are from Spain. During the time of slavery in America and there after, the so-called black people were not allowed to be properly educated or to read, write and learn things to uplift them in the mind. British and United States system of enslavement of the Africans was a non- human legally designated as property. The words used here in the United States black, negro and colored are non- human, Therefore the U.S. legally us these terms as property. (Read the Dred Scott[239] case) In time for those who did were taught to use the Oxford English Dictionary. From The book **Black Labor White Wealth** 1994 Dr. Claud Anderson.[240]

"Since color was the decisive factor in slavery, it was important to know who was and was not a member of the black race. Moors were not classified as members of the black race."

This may share some light of understanding of the history of the name "Moor"

"No longer use Moors or Azenegues but "Negros." "Similarly, in the chronicle of Azurara as soon as the area south of the Senegal river has been reached, where the modern slave trade was begun by Portuguese, the designation of the native Africans is changed from Moors or Azenegues to "negros," which was later transposed into English as "negroes.[241]"

---

[239] March of 1857, the United States Supreme Court, led by Chief Justice Roger B. Taney, declared that all blacks- slaves as well as free were not and could never become citizens of the United States. Because Scott was black, he was not a citizen and therefore had no right to sue for his freedom. The framers of the Constitution, he wrote, believed that blacks " had no rights which the white man was bound to respect; and that a negro might justly and lawfully be reduced to slavery for his benefit. He was bought and sold and treated as an ordinary article of merchandise and traffic, whenever profit could be made by it."

[240] Dr. Claud Anderson , Ed, D. Doctorate of Education degree from Wayne State University.

[241] The "Negro" Its Origin and Evil Use 1960 page 38 by Richard B. Moore (1893-1978) was an African-Caribbean from Barbados, West Indies. civil rights activist .

Keep in mind what is being said here from the past and look into what has been done hereon. The lesson here is, one must truly understand the origin of the word from their own consciousness. This is beyond the adjective of the word black as being Moor, we must think outside of those who may think that it means the same for there is nothing covered that shall not be revealed, and hid that shall not be known.

CHAPTER III

THE MESSAGE

JESUS had said: **"I am the message that I bring to you[242]"** In this new era of time, the message[243] from **Prophet Noble Drew Ali, Savior of Humanity:**

> "Coming as he does with a message for the nations in somewhat the same manner as did Jesus, Mohammed, Buddha, Confucius and other prophets of their day. Only the things of this prophet's day differ from the ills of the days of the past; and yet the remedy for the ills of today is about the same as the remedies for the days past; all turning about the pivot love-Love for humanity[244]" By **Prophet Noble Drew Ali**

Prophet Noble Drew Ali's teaching on religion[245] is the science on religion itself, is the prefix (re) which means again, once more and the root "ligion." is composed from the Latin "ligare" which means to unite,

---

[242] HK of the M. H. T. of S 1927 Chap. 19 Personality Of The Nazarene V28

[243] Message of the Divine of Spiritual thoughts that always bring messages of light (Truth) and teach the way to harmonious co-operation between the indwelling love of the heart and understanding of the mind. Message from the Messenger- Intellectual perception of Truth that cleanses the mind and heart (Soul) and leads to the coming or conscious presence of the indwelling Spirit of Truth.

[244] Moorish Literature is Excerpts taken from the Moorish Guide 1927-1928 Savior Of Humanity

[245] HK of the M. H. T. of S 1927 Chap. 43 The Insufficiency of Knowledge V21 "To what end was religion instituted, but to teach thee thine infirmities, to remind thee of thy weakness.

Greek "legein" which corresponds logic and law.[246] Therefore, one must learn to link their state of mind[247] back to the pure thoughts that they lost in time. This is why it was important for the Prophets to come to redeem their nations from their sinful ways. During those times each Divine Prophet brought what was needed for the people based upon the funda- mental principles of Love, Truth, Peace, Freedom and Justice. The Divine Prophet's did not have a name for their <u>religion it is the way of life</u>. Now, man uses his man made religion theory for the justification of accumulating land and wealth, murder, fear, to control ones thinking and their ways of life. You should realize during the dark ages[248] of Europe through the 5th - 15th century their deep sleep of pure ignorance covering many subjects like religion, science and health etc. Centuries ahead was, a slow wakening process to study and learn from Asiatic cultures. Still they were more inclined to argue about the way they thought life should be. Rather than search and accumulate evidence in order to show what is actually the truth. Later in years when one did actually find the truth, it was covered up or never told.

This was done because, the mind set in Europe was sexism, aggression[249] and superior. Especially the thoughts on religion you see it was said:

"The Christian Church was the handmaiden for the development of racism. While it propagated the theory that all men were crated equal[250] in the sight of God; in practice, it found all sorts of argu-

---

[246] Discover The Key to The Moorish Questionary a study guide for all Moorish Americans 2009 Brother Eric Mungin Bey p. 38 Real religion is based on a certain knowledge of (Know Thyself).

[247] Moorish Literature are Excerpts taken from the Moorish Guide 1927-1928 A Divine Warning By The Prophet For The Nations "I, the Prophet., was prepared by the Great God Allah to warn my people to repent from their sinful ways and go back to that state of mind to their forefathers' Divine and national principles."

[248] Dark Age - Concept of a period of intellectual darkness that occurred in Europe.

[249] The Iceman Inheritance 1978 by Michael Bradley Canadian writer researcher, historian and anthropologist. Princeton Inst. Vanderbilt Univ. York Univ. Yale sch. Of Divinity.

[250] The declaration of Independence - We hold these truths to be self-evident: that all men are created equal.

ments to prove that non-European people, especially Black men, were inferior and could not be considered as men in the general sense."[251]

In the late twenties Prophet Noble Drew Ali was speaking of pride[252] within ones self, This was important in connection with religion because he was bringing our lineage that was disconnected from the past. Prophet Noble Drew Ali was the only one at that time and now who was teaching us to honor all the true and Divine Prophet's.[253] In his book **The Holy Science** 1894 by Swami Sri Yukteswar[254] it will reveal in some what of the same manner teachings as of Prophet Noble Drew Ali's (know Thyself) with a open statement of this book you will clearly understand and see the duties of all Prophets works, words and deeds.

"Prophets of all lands and ages have succeeded in their God-quest. Entering a state of true illumination, These saints have realized the Supreme Reality behind all names and forms. Their wisdom and spiritual counsel have become scriptures of the world. All expressions- some open and clear, others hidden or symbolic-of the same basic truth of spirit."[255]

---

[251] The Iceman Inheritance 1978 also view You Tube (White women tells the Truth about America).

[252] Moorish Literature are Excerpts taken from the Moorish Guide 1927-1928 "If you have race pride and love your race, join the Moorish Holy Temple of Science and become a part of this Divine Movement, then you will have power to redeem your race because you will know who you are and your forefathers were.

[253] It was said from the sages of the past that in the days to come when the name religion was being introduced to replace creed (which means principles of the faith). The truth in the name religion is that you can tell a real religion by one who honors all Divine Prophets.

[254] Jnanavatar Swami Sri Yukteswar Giri (1855 - 1936) He manifested the self-mastery and divine attainment that have been the highest goal of Truth-seekers throughout the ages. His pursuit of Truth led him to the great sage Lahiri Mahasaya 1828-1895 who extolled the sacred science of Kriya Yoga meditation as the most effective means of attaining a universal -realization of our Universal Creator.

[255] The Holy Science 1894 by Jnanavatar Swami Sri Yukteswar Giri These words was foreword in this book by Swami Sri Yukteswar's student Paramahansa Yogananda.

The Purpose of this book **(The Holy Science)** is to show that there is an essential unity in all religions; that there is no difference in the truths inculcated by various faiths; that there is but one method by which the world, both external and internal, has evolved; and that there is but one Goal admitted by all scriptures. Take notice on the front cover of **Prophet Noble Drew Ali's Holy Koran you will see a symbol of a circle seven,** the circle has four breaks[256] each one may be also in connection with **The Holy Science book which is** divided into four sections[257] according to the four stages in the development of knowledge. Prophet Noble Drew said our religion is Islamism,[258] now you must learn that religion here means governmental principle, law and order. Man must have principles that which govern his/her mental state by the knowledge of the Seven Universal laws, then our life will be in harmony (in order)

The message of Islam by Prophet Noble Drew Ali.

> **"Islam is a very simple faith. It requires man to recognized his duties toward God Allah, His Creator and fellow creatures. It teaches the supreme duty of living at peace with one's surroundings. It is preeminently the religion of peace."[259] And "That a follower of Islam in the true sense of the word is one whose hands, tongue and thoughts do not hurt others"**

---

[256] circle 7 which has 4 breaks which means North, East, West and South . Each letter spells out the word News as for the Gospel. The circle also means cycle, which man lives by cycle ages it revolve in 7 (stages) 7 Universal Laws (Mental, Correspondence, Vibration, Polarity, Rhythm, Cause & Effect, Gender).

[257] The four sections are "The Gospel" seeks to establish the fundamental truth of creation, and to describe the evolution and the involution of the world. "The Goal" Existence, Consciousness, and bliss. "The Procedure" deals with the method of realizing the three purposes of life. "The Revelation" discusses the revelations which come to those who have traveled far to realize the three ideals of life and very near their destination. One also must take notice of Buddha's four Noble truths.

[258] Moorish Koran Questionary Q17 What is our religion? Islamism (the "ism" means the condition of being) in which being at peace with the understanding of our scared doctrines.

[259] Moorish Literature are Excerpts taken from the Moorish Guide 1927-1928 p.10 What is Islam?

Be very mindful that if this is not being practiced or lived by nature, then you are not living Islam. In the true since the science of Islam in symbolism is (AS I AM) You need to learn to love[260] instead of hate, one of many sayings of Prophet Noble Drew Ali. The most repeated is the most needed, The True Science of love is, it has the highest energy which is from Allah. From the Sufism[261] message of love:

"Whatever we wish to know well, we must love. We can't master any field of study-whether music, art an academic field, or a profession-unless we love what we are studying. Study without love leads to a shallow, superficial understanding. Real mastery comes from love."

If you love yourself you must study who you are and what you are in order to progress on this earth. This life began with you and you must know the knowledge and wisdom of your higher self[262] and that you must conqueror your lower self.[263]

The highest vibration of the higher self is love and the lower frequency deludes to the lower self. **" The path of love. To love others, to love the beauty of this world develops the capacity for love. The more**

---

[260] The Doctrine of the Sufis 1966 by Arthur John Arberry, M.A. translated from Arabic of Abuced BakrLove is the inclination of the heart, meaning the heart then inclines towards Allah and what is of Allah, with out any effort.

[261] Essential Sufism 1997 edited by James Fadiman & Robert Frager Chapter 11 Love

[262] HK of the M. H. T. of S 1927 Chap. 3 The Unity Of Life V6 "The higher self is human spirit clothed with soul, made in the form of Allah. V8 "The higher self is Allah in man, and will not pass away."V9 " The higher self is the embodiment of truth." V10 " The higher self is justice, mercy, love and right."V11 "The higher self is the mother of the virtues and the harmonies of life."

[263] Ibid. 3 V7 "the lower self, the carnal self, the body of desires, is a reflection of the higher self, distorted by the murky ethers of the flesh. V8 "The Lower self is an illusion and will pass away." V9 "The lower self is truth reversed and so is falsehood manifest. V10 " The lower self is what the higher self is not." V11 " The lower self breeds hatred, slander, lewdness, murder, theft, and everything that harms."

we canlove, the more we can love Allah. To love Allah is to know Allah[264]". Sufism

Prophet Noble Drew Ali said in connection with our religious aims and beliefs:[265]

> "We must promote economic security. The preaching of economic security among us is by no means as widespread and intensive as the circumstances demand. No other one thing is more needed among us at this time than greater economic power. Better positions for our men and women. More business employment for our boys and girls and bigger incomes will follow our economic security." This is important, because he said: "We shall be secure in nothing until we have economic power. A beggar people cannot develop the highest in them, nor can they attain to a genuine enjoyment of the spiritualities of life." We will grow by what we know, you see these lessons of Prophet Noble Drew Ali, Is that we need to grow in our understanding of love so that our mothers can teach these lessons to our little ones, so that they may learn to love instead of hate. And by these lessons our fathers can set our house in order.[266]

The structure of family[267] is very important, because our families will become a conscious nation with a economic security plan for our posterity.

---

[264] Discover The Key to The Moorish Questionary Eric Mungin Bey page 17 Allah is the proper name of The Divine Being, while He is mentioned by a number other names, everyone of which refers to one of His Attributes, Allah comprising all attributes by which He is known. The word God in English language is not A substitute for Allah.

[265] Moorish Literature are Excerpts taken from the Moorish Guide 1927-1928

[266] HK of the M. H. T. of S 1927 p. 3

[267] The Great Learning 500 BC Confucius The ancients who wished to illustrate astonishing virtue throughout the kingdom, first ordered well their own states. Wishing to order well their states, they first regulated their families. Wishing to regulate their families, they fist cultivated their persons. Wishing to cultivate their persons, they rectify their hearts, they first sought to be sincere in their thoughts. Wishing to be sincere in their thoughts, they first extended to the utmost their knowledge. Such extension of knowledge lay in the investigation of things. Things being investigated, knowledge became complete. Their thoughts were sincere. Their thoughts being sincere, their hearts were then rectified. Their hearts being rectified, theirpersons were cultivated. Their persons being cultivated, their

"In order to rightly to govern the state, it is necessary first to regulate the family, it is not possible for one to teach others, while he cannot teach his own family"

Confucius

(Prophet Noble Drew Ali's great program was and is a conscious way towards sovereignty) This is called knowing the root. When applied the resurrection is fact, there is no cutting corners of the plan. If so, there will be unconscious people[268] trying to do the right thing the wrong way. This will only delay the progress of his great program. Nevertheless, love will prevail! Sovereignty comes first from a wise conscious mind based on Prophet Noble Drew Ali's teachings of his Divine principles of Love, Truth, Peace, Freedom and Justice. If these principles are not followed, the worst is yet to come.

"Because the Great God of the Universe is not pleased with the works that are being performed in North America by my people and this great sin must be removed from the land to save it from enormous earthquakes, diseases, etc.[269]"

Noble Drew Ali's thoughts on salvation.[270] Jesus said:

"It has three steps: belief is first, and this is what man thinks, perhaps, is truth. And faith is next, and this is what man knows is truth. Fruition is the last, and this is man himself, the truth. Belief

---

families were regulated. Their families being regulated, their states were rightly governed. Their states being rightly governed, the whole kingdom was made tranquil and happy. These passages all show how those sovereigns made themselves illustrious.

[268] Unconscious people means here is a self deception.

[269] Moorish Literature are Excerpts taken from the Moorish Guide 1927-1928 A Divine Warning By The Prophet For The Nations. Sin which means error (wrongfully thinking).

[270] HK of the M. H. T. of S 1927 Chap. 7 The Meaning Of Truth V27 "Salvation is a ladder reaching from the heart of men to the heart of Allah" Salvation the restitution of man to his spiritual birthright; regaining conscious possession of the universal creator -given attributes. It comes as a result of redemption.

is lost in faith; and in fruition faith is lost; and man is saved when he has reached deific life; when he and Allah are one."

The message here is that, he who stands as the savior or redeemer of one's soul from delusion. The blessing, the intercession, of the real you is of paramount importance.

The real you (spirit man) who is "master of the house" in his unity the inner "door" (soul) to transcendence and salvation. Noble Drew Ali knew that in order for man to be emancipated from his lower thinking he or she must understand the truth about the real teachings of Jesus, that no man can save you. You must save yourself!

The Holy Koran of the Moorish Holy Temple of Science first began with this:

"Know Thyself and Thy Father God Allah. The genealogy of Jesus with his years of events,[271] life works and teachings in India, Europe and Africa, in the land of Egypt.

In connection with Jesus studies one must know that he studied the teachings of Siddhartha Gautama[272] (Buddha) "awakened one" or "the enlightened one"

Buddha's main focus upon human sorrow was that man/woman need the truth[273] for their salvation just as Jesus statement: "Truth shall set you free"

Buddha said: "Truth is one There is no second"

---

[271] The events in the life of Jesus of Nazareth represent certain stages of spiritual growth in natural man.

[272] HK of the M. H. T. of S 1927 Chap. 11 Jesus and Barato-Together They Read The Sacred Books V2 Together Jesus and Barato read the Jewish Psalms and prophets, read the Vedas, the Avesta and the wisdom of Guatama. Buddha 563 BCE born in Lumbini India (today in Nepal) V45 And all the priest gave thanks, and praised the Buddha of enlightenment.

[273] Enlightenment of ones higher self (Love).

Jesus said: "Truth is the only thing that changes not."[274]

Noble Drew Ali "Truth is but one."[275] Prophet Noble Drew Ali was born on the 8th the symbol of infinity[276] the mystical sciences of this, is that Buddha's teachings 8 fold path:

1. <u>Right View</u>   Wisdom
2. <u>Right Intention</u>
3. <u>Right Speech</u>   Ethical Conduct
4. <u>Right Action</u>
5. <u>Right Livelihood</u>
6. <u>Right Effort</u>   Mental Development
7. <u>Right Mindfulness</u>
8. <u>Right Concentration</u>

Which brings us to Prophet Noble Drew Ali's teaching's from **The Holy Koran of the Moorish Holy Temple of Science,**[277] Chapter 8.

"Allah's meeting place with man is in the heart, and in a still small voice He speaks"

Right view - Right intention (wisdom)

"And when man honors man, he honors Allah, and what man does for man he does for Allah. And you must bear in mind that when man harms in thought or word or deed another man, he does a wrong to Allah. If you would serve Allah who speaks with the heart, just serve your near kin, and those who are no kin, the stranger at your gates, the foe who seeks to do you harm. Assist the poor, and

---

[274] HK of the M. H. T. of S 1927 Chap. 7 Jesus Explains To Lamaas The Meaning Of Truth V3

[275] Ibid. Chap. 42 Weakness V23

[276] Something without limits: limitless time, space, or distance. State of being infinite: the state or quality of being infinite.

[277] Jesus Reveals To The People Of Their Sinful Ways p. 13 (13 represent the 1913 the year Prophet Noble Drew Ali begin to reveal his teachings).

help the weak; do harm to none and covet not what is not yours. Then, with your tongue the Holy One will speak; and he will smile behind your tears, will light your countenance with joy, and fill your hearts with peace."

Right Speech - Right Action -
Right Livelihood (ethical conduct)

"When you will offer unto Allah, just take your gift of grain, or meat, and lay it on the table of the poor. From it an incense will arise to heaven, which will return to you with blessedness. Make human hearts your altars, and burn your sacrifices with the fire of love"

Right Effort - Right Mindfulness -
Right Concentration (mental development)

Prophet Noble Drew Ali teaching's is that if you live Chapter 8, then you are a true Moslem.[278] Now, Mohammed[279] the first came upon the scene and fulfilled the works of Jesus of Nazareth.[280] Jesus (Isa) name is mentioned only some thirty-five times in the Holy Qur'an.[281] In numerology 35 - 3+5=8; again we have the symbol of infinity. This is the mastery of above and below (as above also below) each circle top and bottom represent the number 8. The top is infinite and the bottom is finite. When one has mastered this, they have reached a balance in the sciences of life.

---

[278] One who submit to Peace and the divine will of love towards the Universal Creator Allah and his fellow beings.

[279] Mohammed (highly praised) Abu al-Qasim Mohammed Ibn Abd Allah Ibn Ibd Abd Al-Muttalib Ibn Hashim born AD 570 in Mecca. Past at the age of 63 on Monday June 8, 632 in Medina. (PBUH)

[280] HK of the M. H. T. of S 1927 Chap. 46 The Beginning of Christianity

[281] Al-Qur'an is a sacred book of the Muslims/Moslems the word Qur'an is an infinitive noun from the root qara'a meaning, primarily, he collected together things, and also, he read or recited; and the Book is so called both because it is a collection of the best religious teachings.

The original Holy Bible[282] states the prophecy of the coming Prophet Mohammed in John 14:16 Jesus:

"I will pay the Father and He will give another comforter. An apostle who shall come after me who's name shall be Ahmed[283]" (Mohammed).

Of course you will not see it in today's many versions of the Bible, because the original Bible was produced by the African approximately 3, 400 years before the old testament, and more than 4,200 years before the new testament. So! Why is it that today's people are reading a English version with its Roman influence to control the religion of Christianity? Prophet Mohammed message[284] was to bring revelation[285] to the people, the truth about the scared writings of the Holy Bible and its messages.

That is why Prophet Mohammed was known as the Messenger[286] of Allah. His message was clear, there is but one Allah[287] and Mohammed is his Prophet. The first point is that the doctrine of the Divine Unity was restored to its original purity the message of Allah. The Holy Book lays it down that every prophet taught the Unity of Allah[288] and that this

---

[282] A Chronology of the Bible 1973 by Dr. Yosef ben-Jochannan (Dr. Ben) 1918 He was educated in Puerto, Brazil, Cuba, and Spain. Earning degrees in engineering and anthropology also received a doctoral degrees in Cultural Anthropology and Moorish History from the University of Havana and the University of Barcelona, Spain. The very first Bible or Scroll on record produced by the African people of the NileValley was called The Book of the Coming Forth by Day and By Night from the hieroglyphic (scared writings).

[283] Ahmed (highly praised) is a synonym for Mohammed.

[284] HK of the M. H. T. of S 1927 Chap. 19 Personality of The Nazarene V28 "I am the message that I bring to you."

[285] Information revealed of something previously hidden or secret - showing or revealing of divine will or truth. Divine revelation of which the Holy Prophet was recipient.

[286] Messenger - Spiritual thoughts that always bring messages of light and demonstrate the way to a harmonious cooperation between the indwelling love of the heart and understanding of the spiritual knowledge.

[287] HK of the M. H. T. of S 1927 Chap. 35 Religion V1 "There is but one Allah, the author, the creator, the governor of the world; almighty, eternal, and incomprehensible".

[288] Ibid. Chap. 3 The Unity of Life

doctrine was the original basis of all religions. Prophet Noble Drew Ali stated from his **Moorish Guide: Moorish Leader's Historical Message To America**

> "The door of religious freedom made by the American Constitution swings open to all, and people may enter through it and worship as they desire. Without religious freedom, no search for truth would be possible: without religious freedom, no discovery of truth would be useful; without religious freedom, religious progress would be checked and we would no longer march forward toward the nobler life which the future holds for the races of men; without religious freedom, there be no inspiration to lift our heads and gaze with fearlessness into the vast beyond, seeking a hope eternal"

Religious freedom came from the concept of the Moors of Al-Andalus Spain during the dynasty of the Ummayads. They did not force their religion upon the Christians and the Jews, they were all treated with equal respect. Let it be known, that the Moors did not suppress the languages of the people of Al-Andalus, They did not outlaw their sacred customs. Unlike the British and United States system! They did not destroy their legal system, rob them of their political rights, deny them their claim to humanity. The Moors taught that Jesus was a mortal Prophet,[289] appointed for his Divine Mission by the Universal Father Allah. Moorish Andalus was unique among Islamic nations. In Andalus, Moorish women[290] moved freely in public and engaged in various gatherings. The practice of purdah[291] (requirement that women cover their faces in public, etc) was not being practiced. Woman enjoyed more societal freedom than in any other part of the Islamic world. Prophet Noble Drew Ali teaches that we are to uplift

---

[289] Moorish Koran Questionary Q24 Who was Jesus? He was a Prophet of Allah.

[290] Moorish Literature are Excerpts taken from the Moorish Guide 1927-1928 The Prophet said: "Have a deeper appreciation for womanhood."

[291] Purdah or Pardeh (from Persian meaning curtain) is the practice of concealing women from men, which covers the head and neck of a women. Purdah exists in various forms in the Muslim and Hindu followers. India and other cultures.

our women, because she is the soul of a nation, she is our first teacher in life and she represent all the of Love made manifest.[292] Take a very good look at the past and present in many countries under religion, man made laws and customs and notice how these men treat their women, the result is staggering. The horrible acts of injustice committed[293] in the form of man made theories; such belief rest on error and illusion. Based upon an erroneous theological doctrine. One must realize this, that the belief of the majority is not always the correct belief. Humanity must be lifted from the unwholesome depths of poverty, misery and suffering and placed on the solid rock of salvation.[294]

---

[292] HK of the M. H. T. of S 1927 Chap. 1 The Creation And Fall of Man and Chap. 21 V20 "She informeth the minds of her children with wisdom" Chap. 44 Misery V7 "There is but one way to be produce."

[293] HK of the M. H. T. of S 1927 Chap. 43 The Insufficiency of Knowledge V3 "Evil is not requisite to man; neither can vice be necessary to be tolerated; yet how many evils are permitted by the connivance of the laws; how many crimes committed by the decree of the council!"

[294] Moorish Literature are Excerpts taken from the Moorish Guide 1927-1928 p. 9 Savor Of Humanity

These images are displayed because of its visual value of the universal message of love and respect for the feminine energies that has been indoctrinated in the cares of the world, she is fallen humanity that has to be placed back into her proper position. The rock[295] of salvation, that is being demonstrated here is "the rock" which means the knowledge in your faith. This shall determines your salvation, it is through the gnosis (spiritual knowledge) of ones self. Prophet Mohammed the first, the founder of the uniting of Islam, by the command of the great Universal Creator Allah.[296] All Divine prophets did not bring any thing new, they were unifying spiritual knowledge back into the minds of the people that lost their way from the hidden truth. Which leads into an expression of many forms such as

---

[295] HK of the M. H. T. of S 1927 Chap. 7 The Meaning of Truth V19 " Again Lamaas asked: "Of understanding what have you to say?" V20 "And Jesus said: " It is the rock on which man builds himself; it is the gnosis of aught and of naught, of falsehood and truth."

[296] Ibid. Chap. 45 The Divine Origin Of The Asiatic Nations V7

Zoroastrian -ism,[297] Zen,[298] Taoism,[299] Jainism,[300] Hinduism,[301] Sikhism,[302] Bahai[303] and if we look into the principles of the faith of Judaism which said thus: **"believe with perfect faith that all the words of the prophets are true."** This means all Prophets past and presence regardless of their

---

[297] Zarathushtra, or Zoroaster c.630 - 550 BC Persian Prophet - teaches that every single human being dwells the divine essence of our Universal Creator, the divinity in humanity.

[298] Zen is a short for Zen Buddhism - Zen is the Japanese word from the Chinese character "Chan" which origin is from Sanskrit term "dhyana" which means meditation. Paradox is a part of Zen and the teaching of Zen. A paradox nudges your mind into a direction other than the routine. It helps you disengage the rational mind and free up the intuition. It also points to a truth that cannot be rationally derived through the use of logic. Therefore: Zen is nothing and yet everything. Zen is both empty and full. Zen encompasses all and is encompassed by all. Zen is the beginning and the end.

[299] Taoism - Tao which means "The way" originated in China with its various elements such as Yin and Yang symbol which is expressed as everything consisting of a balance, it constitutes reality. It also have given its birth to Tai Chi and Fen-Shui. Tao is defined as the way to the universe.

[300] Jainism is an ancient way of life from India that teaches that the way to liberation and bliss is to live a life of harmlessness and renunciation. The aim of Jain life is to achieve liberation of the soul.

[301] The word Hindu is derived (through Persia) from the Sanskrit word Sindhu, the historic local appellation for the Indus river in the northwestern part of the Indian Subcontinent. its concept of God is complex and depends upon each individual and the tradition and philosophy followed. It is sometimes referred to as henotheistic (i.e., involving devotion to a single creator while accepting the existence of others), but any such term is an overgeneralization. views dharma as the universal principle of law, order, harmony, all in all truth, that sprang first from Brahman.(ultimate power underlying the universe) It acts as the regulatory moral principle of the Universe. Sanātana Dharma, a Sanskrit phrase meaning "the eternal law", or the "eternal way". Also this was the Birth of Yoga.

[302] Sikhism was founded during the 15th century by Guru Nanak April 15 1469 September 22 1539 represented by the phrase of one Universal Creator , who prevails in everything, along with a praxis in which the Sikh is enjoined to engage in social reform through the pursuit of justice for all human beings. Sikh advocates the pursuit of salvation in a social context through the congregational practice of meditation on the name and message of the universal creator. The essence of Sikh teaching is summed up by Nanak in these words: "Realization of Truth is higher than all else. Higher still is truthful living"

[303] Bahá'u'lláh November 12, 1817 May 29, 1892 founder of the Bahai Faith in 19th-century emphasizing the spiritual unity of all humankind. Bahai derived from the Arabic Baha meaning "glory" or "splendor".Three core principles establish a basis for Bahá'í teachings and doctrine: the unity of the Universal Creator, the unity of religion, and the unity of human-kind.

origin. Our Universal Creator only have one creed and that is a Divine Love. Prophet Noble Drew Ali, simply was bringing this knowledge to the people.

>**Moral creed, based on the Authority and Reflection.**
>**The message of Confucius cultivating Reverence.**
>**The message of Mohammed cultivating Faith.**
>**The message of Zoroaster cultivating Purity.**
>
>**Intellectual creed, based on Science and Imagination.**
>**Osirianism (Ancient Egyptians) characterized by Aspiration.**
>**Buddhism characterized by Emancipation.**
>**Brahmanism characterized by Spirituality.**

There are many paths to arrive at the truth, so therefore take on the lessons within the law of learning;

"Accept only that which appeals into your heart as truth, and let the rest pass you by, for the time being-for each comes his own; and none can gain his own, until he is prepared for it." words of the Yogavasishtha from The Spirit of The Upanishads[304]

All of these universal teachings are known as degrees[305] for which one, must learn his or her lessons through the journeys of this life. Although there have been many schools of thought "Know Thyself" was always

---

[304] "The Upanishads" or Sacred writings of India Hindu scripture: any of the sacred texts written in Sanskrit that form the basis for Hindu philosophy and doctrine. They date from the 8th century BC and represent the last stage in the tradition of the Vedas, the most ancient of Hindu scriptures. This information on 1907 "The Upanishads" was reproduced by Yogi Ramacharaka pseudonym or pen-name for William Walker Atkinson born in 1862 Baltimore MD past 1932 William was an attorney, merchant and publisher. He was a associate editor of the Chicago magazine "suggestion" 1900-1905 and then editor "advanced thoughts" 1916-1919 (1903 he began to write books on yoga philosophy.

[305] Moorish Holy Temple of Science Charter from the Prophet Noble Drew Ali states: "Is hereby authorized and empowered to initiate and confer the degrees of said Temple in accordance with the established forms and usages upon all such persons as are duly and lawfully qualified. To promote and practice the teachings of the true and divine prophets: Jesus, Mohammed, Buddha, Confucius, Etc." E means of the earth, T means territory and C means country.

the primary lesson for our Divine creed, Prophet Noble Drew Ali went to study these lessons at an early age and was tested[306] and tried. Before the call of his prophethood he was a student of the Egyptian school thought. Later on in life in due time he received the call to teach the old time religion[307] in which our forefathers are the true and divine founders of our first religious creed, for the redemption and salvation of mankind on earth.[308] Prophet Noble Drew Ali is the founder of the uniting of the Moorish Holy Temple of Science[309] here in North America and his authority is from Allah to propagate the faith and extend the learning and truth. Also establish the faith of Mohammed in America.[310] He said: **"Try to understand what Islamism stands for, and some of the things it has contributed to the world"**[311]

All in essence[312] the deep rooted divine creed came out from ancient Egypt (Kemet) which made its way through many parts of the lands of Asia. Know thyself was the main subject with its teachings of salvation that the soul of man if liberated from its bodily fetters,[313] could enable someone to become into their higher self. Through the centuries we've lost

---

[306] HK of the M. H. T. of S 1927 Chap. 13 Life and Works of Jesus In Egypt V14 " I pray you brothers, let me go into your dismal crypts; and I would pass the hardest of your test."

[307] Ibid. Chap. 48 The End Of Time And The Fulfilling of The Prophesies V3 "Noble Drew Ali: who was prepared and sent to this earth by Allah, to teach the old time religion and the everlasting gospel to the sons of men." This was to know thyself and the gospel were lessons of salvation.

[308] Ibid. Chap. 48 The End Of Time And The Fulfilling of The Prophesies V6

[309] Ibid. Chap. 47 Egypt, The Capital Empire Of The Dominion Of Africa V12

[310] Moorish Koran Questionary Our Authority Corporation-Religious Affidavit of Organization

[311] Moorish Literature are Excerpts taken from the Moorish Guide 1927-1928 p.12 Moorish Leader's Historical Message To America "Mohammedans (Moors) did all in their power to encourage and stimulate research in every branch of human inquiry."

[312] Religion spiritual entity: a spiritual entity.

[313] Restraint: a means of confinement.

this knowledge which has been hidden, manipulated,[314] and restructured[315] by a European concept which would altered your state of mind to confirm to their ideology.[316] But the truth is not lost our ancestors did what they could to ensure that it would not be completely lost. This is the reason why Allah the Universal Creator ordained Noble Drew Ali to teach our divine creed. His teachings based on the Ancient Mystery System which was preserved by the Moors. You may say his teaching is Sufism which is an Islamic group practicing of mysticism that absorb it's way in the 8th and 9th century during the spread of Islam. However, its true origin came out of ancient Egypt (Kemet) Sufi which means wisdom. Prophet Noble Drew Ali's teachings has been misrepresented[317] in many ways and as a result it became to a state of confusion among many. Nevertheless it is in great importance to understand what is Islam? Prophet Noble Drew Ali said this:

> **" Islam is a very simple faith. It requires man to recognize his duties toward God Allah his Creator and his fellow creatures. It teaches the supreme duty of living at peace with one's surroundings. It is preeminently the religion of peace. The very name Islam means peace. The goal of a man's life according to Islam is peace with everything. Peace with Allah and peace with man. A follower of Islam in the true sense of the word is one whose hands, tongue and thoughts do not hurt other"**.[318]

---

[314] Falsify something: to change or present something in a way that is false but personally advantageous.

[315] Change something's basic structure: to change the way in which something is organized or arranged

[316] System of social beliefs: a closely organized system of beliefs, values, and ideas forming the basis of a social, economic, or political philosophy or program.

[317] Give false account of: to give an inaccurate or deliberately false account of the nature of somebody or something and or not represent truly: not to be truly or typically representative of somebody or something.

[318] Moorish Literature are Excerpts taken from the Moorish Guide 1927-1928

NOBLE SOUL 93

The Holy Prophet Moorish Divine[319] and National[320] movement message was re- vealing in its essence, the true nature of spirituality as being the liberation from dogmas[321] and preconceived[322] ideas.[323] The names and symbols in the heading of The Moorish Divine Constitution and by-laws is showing you a way towards Salvation through Allah and Unity.

SALVATION   **ALLAH**   **UNITY**

The star and crescent,[324] an expression that offers a source of inspiration, that will reach a connection with your first eye[325] with the help of the hand press[326] you can therefore use your right and left hemisphere to balance

---

[319] Spiritual Liberty - Divine salvation from an infinite point of view.

[320] National Liberty - Earthly salvation from a finite point of view. relating to or characteristic of a conscious people of a particular nation that is owned maintained, or controlled by central government of a nation. That which will be governed by aggregations of thoughts in the mind that are to be instructed through the faculties.

[321] Group belief: a belief or set of beliefs that a political, philosophical, or moral group holds to be true.

[322] Formed in the mind in advance especially, if based on little or no information or experience and reflecting personal prejudices.

[323] HK of the M. H. T. of S 1927 Chap. 10 Jesus Spake On The Unity Of Allah And Man To The Hindus. V16 "A man's ideal is his God and so , as man unfolds, his God unfolds. Man's God today, tomorrow is not God."

[324] Discover The Key to The Moorish Questionary a study guide for all Moorish Americans 2009 BrotherEric Mungin Bey p. 15 "The star and crescent - we must be the star inside the crescent "it doesn't waver from that spot, is always fixed in steady faith. Therefore, salvation by means of regeneration or trans -formation. The restitution of man to his spiritual birthright.

[325] The first eye is open and receptive only to the guiding light of Spirit. The first eye is the gate that opens to the space of consciousness and inner worlds. It is also the main organ through which the body of energy can be awakened and governed. In practice, the third eye acts as a 'switch' which activates higher states of consciousness and experiences of spiritual vision.

[326] Represents executive ability; the doing of things; outer or manual power. HK of the M. H. T. of S 1927 Chap. 37 "The Breath Of Heaven" V11 "Thine hand, is it not a miracle?

your way of thinking before you act. Because the way you act is the reaction of the way you think, so if you think right, you will act right. The secret of life is balance, and the absence of balance is life's destruction. If you only knew that wisdom is not in words; it is in the knowledge of self, that is why the more man or woman explores him or herself, the more power he or she finds within. Keep this in mind and beware of committing yourself exclusively to a specific belief so that you disbelieve everything else, or else you will miss out on much good-in fact, you will miss out on recognizing authentic truth. You must realize that Prophet Noble Drew Ali offered his teachings to those who were sick at heart, tried for many years, yet they are blind and cannot see the light, nor is the Prophet trying to put new wine in old skins, for he knows that it will burst them. Still he has the remedy for the nations.[327] Words of thoughts from his Religious Controversy written speech, which in some ways will leave you speechless. Simply because of the big and powerful ministers and the trained[328] educated people during those times of the late 20's thought that had the real truth. The fact of the matter is that they have always had only a reflection of the truth and not the real thing. You may say religion is a lesson which teaches the manner of living right and reaching the object[329] for which we are born.[330] Religious creed[331] has come time after time to the world. Through those who have

---

Is there in the creation aught like unto it? Wherefore was it given thee, but that thou mightest stretch it out to the assistance of thy brother?

[327] Moorish Literature are Excerpts taken from the Moorish Guide 1927-1928.

[328] Ibid. " There are but few people who know what the truth is about man, and that few know that it is foolish to try to impart it to the ignorant, Although the ignorant has finished college, he is a fool right on, being trained to jump through a hoop. The longer he stays in schools, the better he can jump. And the more vivid will he defend his jumping."

[329] Moorish Literature are Excerpts taken from the Moorish Guide 1927-1928 "What Is Islam "object of man's life, according to Islam. Is its complete unfoldment."

[330] Ibid. "Islam teaches that man is born with unlimited capacities for progress. Islam does not support the idea that man was born in sin. It teaches that every one has within him the seed of perfect development and it rest solely with himself to make or mar his fortune."

[331] HK of the M. H. T. of S 1927 Chap. 48 "The End Of Time And The Fulfiling Of The Prophesies" V6 "Our forefathers are the true and divine founders of the first religious creed, for the redemption and salvation of mankind on earth."

brought the message of the Universal Creator. Those who came with this message of a religious creed have given it in diverse[332] forms, in accordance with the evolution of the people at that particular time, but the religious creed was one and the same. There never has been any other religious creed than one, for Allah is one, Truth is one, and so the religious creed is one. Look at it like this, If I were to serve water from out one pitcher to four people with four different cups, the stream water which flows from the pitcher and fills its various cups is but one stream of water and so all four different cups of water are one and the same. Prophet Noble Drew Ali's solution to the problem of the day is the awakening of the consciousness of humanity to the divinity of man. When the message of the Universal Creator has given to the world, there was a certain peculiarity in the way it was presented to the world because every messenger was made fit for his own time,[333] and his message suited to that particular time. But behind it all there is one Truth, and one Divine Wisdom in all religions. In realty the message comes from one source and that is from the Universal Creator, so whatever period that message came and in whatever form the message was given, it was always that one message, the message of wisdom through Love. Noble Drew Ali was and is a universal prophet the message that he was bringing was Love, Truth, Peace, Freedom and Justice which was not for one nation, community or a certain group of people; it is for the whole of humanity, Its one and only object is to bring about a better understanding between the divided sections of humanity. But he came to those who call themselves negroes (so call black people) first, because they were the ones that were stripped of their heritage, nationality, language, land, divine creed, mis-educated and dehumanized to the lowest level which has placed us in the belly of the beast. Our people has been separated from the illustrious history of their forefathers who were the founders of the first

---

[332] consisting of different things: made up of many different elements or kinds of things. Differing from each other: or distinct from one another.

[333] HK of the M. H. T. of S 1927 Chap. 48 "The End Of Time And The Fulfilling Of The Prophesies" V1"The last Prophet in these days is Noble Drew Ali, who was prepared divinely in due time by Allah."

civilization of the Old World. This is the reason why we needed a Prophet that was born in North America among his own so that his message can awaken our consciousness to the fact that humanity must be uplifted, so that we may learn the truth about ourselves and take our place back into the families of nations. Take a step away from yourself and behold the path! The source of the realization of the truth is within you; you're the object of your realization. Give yourself some thoughts that has been presented here without emotional judgment whether it's a Prophet or Religion and allow your mind to be the question, and you will find that it is itself its answer. Now remember that reason is the illusion of reality and you are to know that reality itself is its own evidence. You must avoid speculation upon abstract concepts of what some people may say[334] regarding of their various religious beliefs. The truth is well hidden within you,[335] all you need to do is to think for yourself without any influence from outside sources that may change your way of thinking or your understanding of the truth. All Divine Prophets are Manifestations of Truth. His Divine Prophet **Confucius** was to develop the education of the knowledge of Truth. His Divine Prophet Buddha provided emancipation to deliver the mind to the absolute truth. His Divine Prophet **Yoseph** (Jesus) spread the Gospel of the Truth. His Divine Prophet **Mohammed** established the Faith in Truth. His Divine Prophet **Noble Drew Ali** confirmed the Truth. All chosen Ones of the Universal Creator proclaimed the Truth. Truth is the oneness of the kingdom of humanity in which its final goal is our Spirutual destiny. They all were here to send a message to the people to unfold to our spiritual nature for our well being.

> **"He who does not travel will not know the value of men."**
> (Moorish saying)

---

[334] HK of the M. H. T. of S 1927 Chap. 38 The Soul Of Man V27 "General opinion is no proof of the truth, for the generality of man are ignorant."

[335] Ibid. Chap. 37 The Breath Of Heaven V1 Vaunt not thy body; because it was first formed; nor of thy brain, because therein thy soul resideth. Is not the master of the house more honorable than its walls?

With that in mind lets travel into our illustrious history to get a basic understanding of our national identity[336] (Moorish American) But first lets understand that the word value here means principles or standards: The accepted principles or standards of an individual or a group. Allow yourself to review Prophet Noble Drew Ali's divine principles (Love, Truth, Peace, Freedom and Justice). A group as a number of people or things considered together or regarded as belonging together and or people with something in common: A number of people sharing something in common such as an interest, belief, or political aim. "Moorish Divine National Movement, which is incorporated in this government and recognized by all nations of the world.[337]" In order for nations to recognize the name Moorish American there must be some history or linkage to their forefathers. Prophet Noble Drew Ali mention Ham[338] in his Holy Koran who was the inhabitant of Afru-ika which means Motherland from The ancient Egyptian language. This term was used to designate beginnings, referring to inner Afru-ika, the place the ancestors of the ruling class came from. Later the Romans Latinized this word to Africa, and the adjective for Africa is 'Afer', which, means 'black', dark. Notice that all Europeans (outsiders) always Identified our people with an adjective, where as we identified ourselves according to the attributes of our Universal Creator, visions of our lands and our ways of life. Thus all lands has been Nationalized before European invasions, so how did this whole continent get its name? The name of Africa comes from a man they call Leo Africanus who's real name was Al-Hassan ibn Mohammed al Wazzani;[339] he was a Moor

---

[336] Here is the science behind identity (entity) a real being whether in thought (as an idea conception) or in fact: being; essence; existence. This is in relation to our nationality card were it states "this is your nationality and identification card" an ID which states who you are. With this you must absolutely know your state of being , your true essence and acknowledge of your existence through your ancient forefathers. Prophet Noble Drew Ali knew that we needed a national identity which is recognized by all nations.

[337] Moorish Literature are Excerpts taken from the Moorish Guide 1927-1928 A Divine Warning By The prophet For The Nations.

[338] Ham as a Nationality (30 Nations came out of Ham).

[339] Born either 1493 or 1494 in the city of Granada Spain and lived in Fes Morocco.

and Moslem from Morocco. He was a traveler[340]-historian[341] and at various times, a diplomat, jurist, hospital administrator, geographer, and teacher. He served under two Sultans and popes during his time, he was a man of many levels and no one disputes the value of his writing about his book that was published in Venice in 1550. He was an ambassador for Sultan Askia Muhammad I (1493-1538) under the Songhai Empire.[342] Leo traveled from Timbuktu to Hausa land (now eastern Mali and southern Niger) across the neighboring kingdoms of Borno (now northeastern Nigeria) and Kanen (now in Chad and Libya), on up through Egypt, along the Nile to Aswan. He kept a meticulous[343] account of everything he saw, smelled, tasted and heard and attention to detail. Returning in June of 1518 by sea from Constantinople, his ship was attacked by Christian pirates who rob Muslim ships and selling captives into slavery. By recognizing this Moor of learning, as evidenced by the various maps and charts and so they determined that this well-spoken Moor might be of more use to the Pope Leo X than to the slave traders. Once he arrival in Rome he became a prisoner in a short term because he found himself faced with a choice of conversion and freedom versus indefinite imprisonment. And so Leo was baptized on January 6, 1520 by the pope himself, who christened his new convert name " Johannes Leo de Medicis." or "Giovanni Leone.[344]" In later years he gained his freedom and proclaim his original name and religion. It was said that Shakespeare may have used Leo as Othello, because there were numerous similarities in the back stories of each figure. He never used the name Leo Africanus, it was used after his death. Because he brought the knowledge to Europe about Afru-ika they called him by his Christian

---

[340] In the course of his travel from Timbuktu to Istanbul, he survived Atlas mountain blizzards and Nile crocodile attacks.

[341] He gained fame while in Italy for his knowledge of the Maghrib, or North Afru-ika, and the Afru-ikan interior, which he set down in a book called The History and Description of Afru-ika and the Notable things therein contained.

[342] Also known as Songhai Empire located in western Afru-ika from the 15th to the 16th century.

[343] Extremely careful and precise.

[344] Arabic version of his new name Yuhanna al-Asad -John the Lion.

name Leo and add Africanus, And now he was known as Leo Africanus. As I mentioned in the footnote that Al-Hassan Ibn Mohammed Al Wazzani was born in Granada which was in Spain, However his parents proclaim him as being a Moor and not a Spaniard. I guess you are thinking how could this be, well for some reason we think that when we are born we get our nationality from the land, to some degree yes, but its much more deeper than that. In ancient times nations did not relate to geographical origin but rather to birth. Nation in a traditional meaning Ancient Civilized Societies usually mean identification with autonomous[345] City-State[346] or a Monarch.[347] The science here is to learn that before the word nationality was first used by 1784-91. Ancient Civilized Societies was recognized by their origin of birth within their clan or tribe. Therefore, When Prophet Noble Drew Ali said to proclaim Moorish as your nationality, he is teaching you to proclaim your Moorish Ancestry.[348] Here is a fascinating view, by the Moors having so much knowledge with a higher culture of life in their society. The Noble Families in Europe's coats of arms or family crest was a way to trace their families back to the Moorish ancestry. The coats of arms will demonstrate their Moorish ancestry in French, Dutch, Belgian, Italian, Spanish, Polish, German, and Portuguese. There are fifty or more variations of the word Moor in the European Languages. Maurice, Maury, Moran, Moore, Morris. This was possible because the Moors brought light

---

[345] Autonomy - Auto-prefix means "self" and nomy suffix refers to "laws" - Independence or freedom as the condition of being autonomous; self -government community. The capacity of a agent to act in harmony with objective morality rather than under the influence of desires.

[346] City-State - an autonomous state consisting of a city and surrounding territory.

[347] Monarch - A sovereign head of State a Sultan, Emperor or Empress. One that reigns over a large piece of land like territory or state. Monarch means one ruler, in a republican state, the ruler or head is often elected for a period of time. HK of the M. H. T. of S 1927 Chap 29 Magistrate And Subject V1 "O thou, The favorite of Heaven, Whom the sons of men, thy equals, have agreed to raise to sovereign power and set as a ruler over themselves; consider the ends and importance of their trust, far more than the dignity and height of thy station."

[348] Ancestors: Forefathers. Those who think of themselves as descended from human ancestors. somebody's ancestors regarded as a line linking the modern generation to its past.

into Europe and with its governing class the Europeans thought marriage or mating with the Moors was an honor. In America history our people of whom was known as negro, black, and colored was never to be taught of their Moorish ancestry from their slave masters laws. The people in America who proclaim their nationality; like the Greeks, Italians, Chinese, Japanese and English are acknowledging their ancestral[349] history of their forefathers, this was as act of honor and respect. Look at the history of the Dutch[350] nationality which is somehow related to Germany as both were part of the Holy Roman Empire of German Nations about 500 years ago. In Dutch the country is called 'Nederland' now spelled Netherlands in its entirety is often referred to as "Holland." The Dutch Empire[351] comprised the overseas territories controlled by the Dutch Republic and later, the modern Netherlands from the 17th century to the mid-1950's.

Although, there is no name of a country called Dutch but there are people in American who proclaim their nationality as Dutch American.[352]

Here is a list of notable Dutch Americans, including both original immigrant who obtained American citizenship and Americans of full or partial Dutch ancestry.

---

[349] Of previous generations: belonging to former generations of somebody's family, or inherited from them.

[350] Dutch - The origins of the word Dutch go back to proto-Germanic, the ancestor of all Germanic languages, official language of the Netherlands and the Republic of Suriname, and one of the West Germanic group of Indo-European languages. 14th century. From Middle Dutch dutsch, from a prehistoric Germanic word meaning "people," which is also the ancestor of English deutsche mark and Teuton.

[351] Dutch Empire - The Dutch followed Portugal and Spain in establishing an overseas colonial empire. The Dutch initially built up colonial possession on the basis of indirect state capitalist corporate colonialism, via the Dutch East and west India Companies. Dutch exploratory voyages revealed vast new territories to Europeans.

[352] Dutch Nationality - The history of Dutch nationality is the going out of sense of national identity in the region of the Netherlands. Consciousness of national identity was manifested through shared national obligations and rights such as tax, martial duty, political and sociable rights, but most of importantly through the notion of citizenship. What is black Dutch nationality? It was said that "Black Dutch" were dark-complexioned Germans or Dutch; also loosely applied to dark-complexioned American of European descent. Something to really think about.

Christina Aquiler Female singer, Dutch ancestry.

Humphrey Bogart (1899-1957) His father was Dutch descent. The name "Bogart" comes from the Dutch surname "Bogaert." which means "orchard."

Marlon Brando (1924-2004) male actor, father was of partial Dutch ancestry.

Robert De Niro male actor, his mother was Dutch ancestry.

Clint Eastwood male actor, Dutch ancestry.

Angelina Jolie female actress, Her mother has Dutch ancestry.

Kris Jenner previously know as Kardashian; She has Dutch ancestry.

Franklin D. Roosevelt (1882-1945), Democratic President of the U.S. Roosevelt is an Anglicized form of the Dutch surname 'Van Rosevelt' or 'Van Rosenvelt', meaning from field of roses.

Anderson Cooper CNN journalist, mother is Dutch American socialite Gloria Vanderbilt.

Bruce Springsteen singer song writer, his father, Douglas Frederick Springsteen, was of Dutch ancestry. His surname in Dutch means jumping stone.

Jack Nicholson male actor, mother was Pennsylvania Dutch[353] descent._

Now to say that Moorish American is not a nationality is like a great grandson denying his great grandfather and great grandmother ever existed. The mystical sciences that is demonstrated here, is that Prophet Noble Drew Ali completely understood the importance of family structured societies that produce a nation with a common interest of a spiritual concept of evolving the true self, in order to sustain[354] this mortal life here on earth. Most so-called African Americans may say that they are mix with

---

[353] German and Swiss immigrants in Pennsylvania: a group of people who emigrated from Germany and Switzerland to eastern Pennsylvania in the 17th and 18th centuries, or their descendants.

[354] Sustain - nourish: to provide somebody with nourishment or the necessities of life and provide to keep somebody going with emotional or moral support.

European, Native American Indian, Mexican ancestry etc. and some make statements; like I don't know my ancestry linkage because my people were taken out of Africa and brought to America as slaves. It was known that out of one blood[355] created all people, these people originally are from Afru-ika (mother-land.) The original blood represents the principle of eternal life with its spiritual potency. In this respect it became part of the spiritual life of the human being. So to say that you are mixed, you have to acknowledge your first blood of your origin to define of who you really are. In regards to as being told that our ancestors was brought from Afru-ika and it is impossible to determine geographically who you are descendant from. Lets keep in mind that our ancestors came out from Afru-ika and migrated throughout the land and develop empires one was the Ghana Empire[356] of western Sudan.[357] Ghana means both "warrior king and king of gold." The

---

[355] Blood - vital life force: blood considered as a vital life force. family or kinship: family background or descent from a particular ancestor, especially when viewed as determining a person's character or appearance. The name of the origin of the key to civilization in regards to type of blood is O (type) the Omeans original. The long experience with slavery and later with Jim Crow segregation in the South the term of the One drop blood rule came into affect. A single drop of "black blood" makes a person black. Which means who was consider to be a so-called negro or black person. It is also known as the "one black ancestor rule," some courts have called it the "traceable amount rule," meaning that racially mixed persons are assigned the status of the subordinate group. This definition emerged from the American South to become the nation's definition, generally accepted by the so-called whites and the so-called blacks. "You are to be reminded that black, negro, colored and mulatto were slave terms for the slave master's property" The term "mulatto " was used to mean the offspring of the so-called pure African Negro and a so-called pure white. The root meaning of mulatto, in Spanish, is "hybrid," mulatto came to include the children of the unions between the so-called whites and so-called "mixed Negroes."

[356] The ancient empire of Ghana c750 -1240 founded by the people called Soninke which means " followers of Sunni or people from the of Sonni" (1st ruler of Ghana was Dingha Cisse) The Soninke people belonged to a larger language group called Mande. The Mande people was aboard the Amistad (watch 1998 the movie Amisad.) Empire location - West Afru-ika The Mande people were the ancient Moabites (Moors).

[357] The original term "Sudd", from the modern term "Sudan" is derived, refers to a vast expanse of floating water plants or swamps. The earliest mention of the word "Sudd" in reference to modern Sudan appear in the writings of Seneca, who recorded an expedition sent by the Roman Emperor Nero to central Sudan. Later in history, Arab writer, unaware of the origin of the word " Sudan", interpreted the term as being derived from the Arabic

ancient Nubians referred their land as "Ka" of which the name "Kush.[358]" The name "Nubia," which is widely used To designate the people of Kush, is synonymous with the terms "Nobae" or Noba". (nobility- family, birth, title, rank, and eminence) The later were Nilo-Saharan[359]

People who dominated Kush beginning in the third century AD. Since "Nubia was a source of gold to the ancient Egyptians, some historians speculate that the term may have originated from the Egyptian word "Nub" meaning "gold".[360] A new and more powerful empire rose in Ghana's place, The Mali Empire[361] of West Afru-ika.[362] Mali means "where the King[363] resides" The next was the Songhai Empire,[364] one of the largest Islamic Empire In history of the sub-Saharan Afru-ika has ever seen. The Songhai society was highly structured, comprising a king and nobility, free

---

word" Soud", meaning "Blacks." this is a very good example of misinterpreting the name Moor or Moorish as being black.

[358] HK of the M. H. T. of S 1927 Chap. 47 Egypt, The Capital Empire of The Dominion of Africa V2 "Old man Cush and his family are the first inhabitants of Afru-ika who came from the land of Canaan."

[359] Central-African language family: a family of around 100 languages spoken in some central parts of Afru-ika, the major branches of which are Chari-Nile, Nilotic, and Saharan. About 15 million people speak one of the Nilo-Saharan languages.

[360] From a metaphysically point of view, gold represents spiritual gifts; the riches of Spirit. The gold that is the consciousness of the omnipresent riches of substance. We must charge our mind with wise and rich ideas. HK of the M. H. T. of S 1927 Chap. 27 The Holy Unity of The Rich And The Poor V1 The man to whom Allah hath given riches, blessed with a mind to employ them aright, is peculiarly favored and highly distinguished.

[361] The Ancient Empire of Mali 1200s -1400s founded by the people called Mandinkas, Malinkes, or Mandingoes. (Mali also called Mande or Mandigo)

[362] Western part of Afru-ika below the Sahara desert near the Niger river.

[363] From a metaphysically point of view, King (righteous) The executive faculty in every man whose life is guided, governed, and directed by Spirit. Mali's greatest King Mansa Musa, who ruled from 1307-1332The word Mansa refers to king, emperor, chief, or sultan. The name Musa means Moses.

[364] The Ancient Empire of Songhai or Songhay, which is a member of a group of people, living along the Niger River in Mali, extending from the Lake Debo through Niger to the mouth of the Sokoto River in Nigeria. There are a form branch of the Nilo-Saharan language of the Kushite family. Sonni Ali the first Emperor of Songhai Empire 1464-1493.

commoners (ordinary person: an ordinary member of society[365] who does not belong to the nobility) The empire flag was a red flag with a five pointed solid green star in the center.[366] What they all have in common was geographically in the Sahara[367] area. The Sahara cover large parts of Algeria, Chad, Egypt, Libya, Mali Mauritania, Morocco, Niger, Western Sahara, Sudan and Tunisia. It is one of three distinct <u>physiographic provinces</u>[368] of the Afru-ika massive physiographic division. In all these lands the Moors (human beings) with many Tribes, Clans with such names as Moab<u>ite</u>, Canaan<u>ite</u>, Hitt<u>ite</u>, Amor<u>ite</u> brethren who sojourned from the land of Canaan seeking new homes.[369] Brethren (members of the same family, group, class, or community). (ite) is a suffix that means member of the tribe, one connected with or descended from.[370] Also the inhabit-

---

[365] HK of the M. H. T. of S 1927 Chap. 30 Social Duties V1 "Placed thee in the society to receive and confer reciprocal helps and mutual obligations, protection from injuries, thy enjoyment of the comforts and the pleasures of life: all these thou oweth to the assistance of others, and couldst not enjoy but in the bands of society".

[366] Moorish Koran Questionary 1928 Q19 What kind of flag is the Moorish ? It is a red flag with a five pointed green star in the center. Note* this star is a open star this was to be as an expression of Scared geometry of Moorish Science bringing its infinite stages into existence. The true high science of Sovereignty on a Divine level.

[367] Sahara means "desert" Sahel means " shore" This was know as "Sea of sand" and the camels are called "ships of the deserts" Note* The two hump camel originated in North America about four million years, they spread across to South America, Afru-ika and Asia.

[368] Physiographic province is a geographic region with a specific geomorphology and often specific subsurface rock type or structural elements. A continent may be subdivided into various physiographic province, each having a specific character, relief, and environment which contributes to its uniqueness.In the Western United States of western North America (Noble Drew Ali's teaching of The North Western shores of Afru-ika) Utah, Colorado, Arizona, Nevada, Central Valley (California) are physiographic province example. Note*All the original names of these lands were in ancient Mexico. The name Moab means "Beautiful land" Moab a city in Utah name after a tribe called Ute. Note* see p.30 Grand Canyon and p. 40 Moorish looking head found within Mexico. In Utah the Navajo were the descendents of a people they called Anasazi (a Navajo word meaning " the ancient ones) remember the book When Rocks cry out, The First Americans were Africans and They Came Before Columbus.

[369] HK of the M. H. T. of S 1927 Chap. 47 V6

[370] Prophet Noble Drew Ali's Divine Constitution and By -Laws Act 7 The Moorish American are the descendants of the ancient Moabites who inhabited the Northwestern and Southwestern shores of Africa.The ancient Moabites spoke the Canaanite language.

ants of land in which they came from or lived. It is a well known fact that the slave trade was from the location of West Afru-ika, The same location of all the empires. Some of these people who was brought from West Afru-ika to the Americas and the islands with many tribal names were of Moorish descent. This explains why Prophet Noble Drew Ali said that our nationality is Moorish American, he was proclaiming of our ancient forefathers names. The suffix in (ity) nationality means state of being, as in a state of being a nation.[371] In other words we belong to an industrious tribe or clan of human beings. If we go back before the height of the Egyptian Empire at the period in West Afru-ikan history and even before, civilization was in its fullest stage of development in the Western Sahara in what is known today Mauritania.[372] One of Afru-ika's earliest civilizations,[373] the Zingh Empire,[374] existed and many have lived in what was lake filled, wet and fertile Sahara, were ships criss-crossed from place to place. They expanded their trade to the Americas, where the evidence for an ancient Afru-ikan presence is over-whelming. A number of large kingdoms and empires existed in the area of the regions from the coast of West Afru-ika to the South, all the way inland to the Sahara. Trade[375] was our way of life local and international therefore our forefathers migrated into many parts throughout the land. Some preserve the same customs, clothing, language or develop a new language out from our old language.

---

[371] Nation - suffix (tion) means action of, state of. Which mean action of the people or state of the people.

[372] Mauritania means land of the Moors.

[373] HK of the M. H. T. of S 1927 Chap 45 The Divine Origin Of The Asiatic Nations V2 "The key of civilization was and is in the hands of the Asiatic nation."

[374] One of the oldest empires and civilization on earth existed just north of the coastal region into what is today Mauritania. It was called the Zingh Empire and was highly advanced. In fact they were the first to use the red, black and green flag and to plant it throughout their territory all over Afru-ika and the world.

[375] HK of the M. H. T. of S 1927 Chap. 47 "Egypt, The Capital Empire of The Dominion of Africa" V8"The River Nile was dredged and made by the ancient Pharaohs of Egypt, in order to trade with the surrounding kingdoms. Also the Niger River was dredged by the great Pharaohs of Egypt in those ancient days for trade , and it extends eastward from the River Nile, westward across the Great ATLANTIC. It was used for trade and transportation." The Mississippi River, The Ohio, in North America.

To say that you are of Moorish decent is acknowledging the connection of your ancient Canaanite, Moabite, Kushite, Kamite (Ham) Mande, Dogon, and XI (Olmec) etc… ancestors, which is all recorded in our DNA. By doing so you have finally linked yourself to the families of nations.

THE MYSTICAL SCIENCE ORIGIN OF EI AND BEY

As Jesus and Barata read the scared books we learn the following from Allah's own record book we read:[376]

> **"The Triune[377] Allah breathed[378] forth, and stood seven spirits his face. The Hebrews call these seven spirits Elohim[379]. And these are they who, in their moved boundless power, created everything that is, or was. These spirits of the Triune Allah moved on the face of boundless space and seven[380] others were and every other had its form of life. These forms of life were but the thought of Allah, clothed in the substance of their ether planes. These planes with all their teeming thoughts of Allah are never seen by eyes of man**

---

[376] HK of the M. H. T. of S 1927 Chap. 11 - The 11 is a master number it means "The Psychic Master" the mystical science here is "As Above" which represents infinite and "So Below" that represents a finite point of view. All are meant to be of service: "As Above" in a spiritually way, or "So Below" in a material or physical way.

[377] Ibid. Chap. 10 "The Unity of Allah and Man" V14 "This Universal Allah is wisdom, will and love." V15 "All men see not the Triune Allah, One see him as Allah of might, another as Allah of thought, another as Allah of love." Father (Masculine/will) - Mother (Feminine/wisdom) = Love: all are pure energy

[378] Breathed - The inspiration of Spirit; the silent movement of the Universal Creator within our being. which became the soul of the man manifestation, includes all emotions and energies that move in and through the organism, and it is always designated as feminine.

[379] Elohim - Elohim thus represents the universal Principle of Being that designed all creation. The material universe is created from the energies of the seven rays, and this is done by reducing the vibration of the rays by a certain factor. A mental blueprint is then superimposed upon this energy on order to form the basic structures that make up the material universe. There is a masculine/feminine polarity at this level.

[380] They were known by other names such as "The seven Rays" " The seven eyes of Allah" and "The Ascended Masters."

in flesh; They are composed of substance far too fine for fleshy eyes, and still they constitute the soul of things."

During the ancient continent of Mu,[381] that led to legendary story "Secret of The Andes"[382]

"The race the original true man, were called Cyclopean,[383] and are known in the secret, arcane knowledge as the 'L' Race or simply, the Els.' Before coming to Earth planet they traversed space following all the great cycles of Time. They were the first life upon the Earth and are Immortals of the legends, God Race or Elder Race that preceded man."

"The Els were not known by that name until they achieved this Theta[384] condition. It was their method of leaving physical existence and conditions that gave them the name of El. Through the secret use of the Ninety Degree[385] Phase Shift they abandoned the Earth and Left it vacant for humanity."

The ancient ones were known as the El-der[386] Race. Currently used

---

[381] Mu pronounce Moo / Lemuria, advanced civlilization in the pacific ocean.

[382] Secret of the Andes 1961 by Brother Philip - Be very mindful if you read this book of its truth and falsehood strangely mix. Take the useful information of what you can and let the rest pass you bye.

[383] Cyclopean / Cyclops - Third eye / seaching quality of mind with keen observation that selects only that which is good. The single eye is open and receptive only to the guiding light of Spirit. (Pineal gland).

[384] They conquered physical matter and became Gods. They annihilated Time and Space; no longer did they need of the Earth world. They were free! They became true members of the Thought Universe, Theta Universe.

[385] A ninety-degree angle forms the letter 'L.' Therefore, when we call them El we are referring to a symbol of there race and not really to a name. L is the 12 symbol. In numerology it is a 3, the number of creativity.

[386] El means "the strong and ever-sustaining One," attribute of Allah. EL - Creators of energy / El today will be used as God/Goddess. So we, some what coming into a light of understanding to call ourselves Gods & Goddesses. Origin of these words are from a European concept of the idea of god. Prophet Noble Drew Ali gave this lesson of this

today in reference to one who is older and you know that old saying respect your elders. What this really means is to honor your father and mother.[387] Look at some of the words that came from out of the root word[388] El: elate, electric, electron, elegant, element, elevate, eleven, elixir and eloquence. All meaning of those words has a radiant Effect and El was the Cause. (7 Universal laws of Cause & Effect) Brother I Cook Bey said that Prophet Noble Drew Ali stated that:

> "I remember when I was on the soul plane, I did not want to come here, but My Father sent Me."

With such an elated statement, we have to observe the following mystical science to this message. Let us unveil the 5th book of Revelation[389] first 5 verses.

1. **And I saw in the right hand of him that sat on the throne a book written within and on the backside, sealed with seven seals.**
2. **And I saw a strong angel proclaiming with a loud voice, Who is worthy to open the book, and to loose the seals thereof?**

---

from the HK of the M. H. T. of S 1927 Chap. 3 The Unity Of Life "and yet these gods possess no ear to hear, no eyes to see, no heart to sympathize, no power to save. This evil is a myth; these gods are made of air, and clothed with the shadow of a thought." Remember god is a title.

[387] Ibid. Chap. 48 The End Of Time And The Fulfilling Of The Prophesies V9 The covenant of the great God-Allah: "Honor thy father and thy mother that thy days may be longer upon the earth land, which the Lord thy God, Allah hath given thee!" note* Prophet Noble Drew Ali was teaching us in the language that we only knew so God-Allah and Lord thy God was a learning tool to get us to comprehend in our minds that when we see or hear the word god he means Allah. Once we can connect that degree we will know longer use the word god.

[388] Root word - The root of the word carries the main meaning of the word.

[389] Revelation - Divine revelation is much more common than is understood. The Spirit of truth is revealing the hidden wisdom to thousands on every hand.

3. **And no man in heaven, nor in earth, neither under the earth, was able to open the book, neither to look thereon.**
4. **And I wept much, because no man was found worthy to open and to read the book, neither to look therein.**
5. **And one of the elders saith unto me, Weep not: behold, the Lion of the tribe of Judah, the Root of David, hath prevailed to open the book, and to loosen the seven seals thereof.**

1. Is this the book of the circle 7 ?
2. Do we accept him as an angel of Allah?
3. Has anyone before the Prophet came to revel the book of the seven seals?
4. Was He the servant who was worthy of his hire?

> Now we have arrived at the plane of the Elders.[390] The (Lion) the one who has enough courage for Truth who was to come out from the (tri-be) an inhabited place within the trinity from which Judah[391] represent. From the root of David which mean "beloved one" David[392] represent the powerful and ancient thought form to which they have access.

---

[390] The El-ders were responsible for 19 of the unsolved mysteries that still ponder some scholars and archeologists today, such as the mystical sciences from the people of Mu & Atlantis, the Olmecs (XI) founders of the American civilization, PSI- The sciences of seeing the unseen, The Mayas, The secret of Tutankhamen's Mummy, Iron Pillar, Bermuda Triangle, Stonehenge, The Pyramids, The Jungle of Angkor and Reincarnation.

[391] Judah - The Mystical science of the name is a teacher. The elements are earth and ether - the practical and the ideal, the spiritual and the physical. The one who will come to give their expression to basic life energies with new fire. They have a great capacity for spiritual aspiration. A teacher that can see and experience the ideal and concept, and at the same time translate it so that others can work within their own lives, in their own manner. Avatar - "descent" (of a deity to the earth in incarnate form).

[392] HK of the M. H. T. of S 1927 Chap. 3 The Unity of Life V23 "The David of the light is purity, who slays the strong Goliath of the dark, and seats the savior, love, upon the throne."

5. Did not the Prophet open the book of the seven seals to you?

The 5 is to demonstrate the divine principals of Love, Truth, Peace, Freedom and Justice. This is a very important affirmation because of the energy it gives.

Once you have absorb all its contents to the fullest you have arrived at the door step to the Restitution of man to his spiritual birthright.

"It will be through his work that humanity will be brought from the slime of life and placed on the solid rock of salvation" by Prophet Noble Drew Ali

"Great work of master minds is to restore the heritage of man, to bring him back to his estate that he had lost, when he again will live upon the ethers of his native plane."[393]

Through the cycle[394] ages we now have come to the Ascened Masters, who were to be spiritually enlightened beings who in past incarnations were ordinary humans, But who have undergone a series of spiritual transformations originally called initiations. The 4th one of the 7th Ascened Masters was Serapis Bey, he was from the realm of Bey,[395] hence the name, wherein is His dwelling place. Who was Serapis Bey?

The Spiritual Hierarchy
The 9 orders of angelic beings
(1 being the highest order)

---

[393] HK of the M. H. T. of S 1927 Chap. 11 Jesus and Barata-together they read the sacred books V36

[394] Cycle or Circle - which is a series of events (a process) that repeats itself endlessly.

[395] Realm of Bey - was another term used for Dominions which mean "Supreme authority, sovereignty" The Dominions are the heavenly beings who govern the activities of all the angelic groups lower than they are. They also serve to integrate the spiritual and material worlds, their work is connected to your reality. Dominion is an inner consciousness obtained only through mind discipline. This supreme authority comes as man realize his oneness with the Universal Creator. Bey - govern energy

The First Sphere- angels who serve as heavenly counselors

1. Seraphim
2. Cherubim
3. Thrones

The Second Sphere- angels who serve as heavenly governors

4. Dominions - Serapis Bey
5. Virtues
6. Powers

The Third Sphere- angels who serve as heavenly messengers

7. Principalities
8. Archangels
9. Angels - Noble Drew Ali

He came as a guardian to Earth's evolutions, and took physical embodiment as many did. Serapis Bey is the Chohan[396] of the 4th Ray, to be a Chohan of the Seven Rays means, the energy of that ray from the heart of Allah was full ordained to be the Lord of the plane of soul, and of the plane of things made manifest. The 4th Ray is the White or Crystal Ray of purity, discipline, and joy. It is the ascension Flame, and the White Light of the Mother in the Base of the spine Chakra. Serapis works With spiritual seeker to help them develop the qualities of Purity, Hope, Discipline, excellence and in gaining mastery over the lower self. This was the origin of the Sacred Schools of the Prophets and The Silent Brother Hood. Serapis Bey is the master energy healer whose work is based in focused intent,[397]

---

[396] Chohan - is a Sanskrit word for "Lord"

[397] The mystical science is that the individual must have a conscious control through his thought and feeling to govern the atomic structure of his own body is to understand the One Principle Governing form throughout Infinity. When man will make the effort

reading and directing energy. His works in time expanded to the people in Mu, Atlantis and Egypt.

"The Turks[398] are the true descendants of Hagar,[399] who are the chief protectors of the Islamic Creed of Mecca"[400]

Indeed Prophet Noble Drew Ali give us the highest names on earth, both of these names holds the symbol of E.[401] The E gives one opportunities to develop universal consciousness within the physical life inherent with all its abilities. It invokes the highest form of intuition. E sounds a vibration that opens true clairvoyance, also awaken the ability to comprehend. The short E sound in Bey activates the throat chakra. This is the center of higher creativity that can enable one to bring the thoughts out of the ethereal realm of the mind into physical manifestation.[402] E sound El (eel) not L, the Long E sound is one that gives the individual opportunity to activate two chakra centers-the brow (third eye) and the crown. Both centers of the head and throat, they all reflect lessons and abilities in

---

to prove this to himself or within his atomic flesh body, he will then proceed to Master Himself. When he has done that, all else in the Universe is his willing co-worker to accomplish whatsoever he will through Love.

[398] Ottoman Turkish - Turks and Persian adopted the name Bey as a title for chieftain, traditionally applied to the leaders of small tribal groups. Bey, Beg, Bek, Bai, Baj, Baig or Beigh. They are all the same word meaning of "Lord." The regions or provinces where Bey's ruled which they administered were called Beylik meaning "governorate."

[399] Hager -is more than a name; it is a title derived from the Egyptian name Hag or Heg a pre-dynastic matriarchal ruler and Holy Women of either ancient Kush or Egypt, who spoke the words of power. Later, this queen name was used to identify any wise women or high priestess, "Hag" and "Wise, HolyWomen" became synonyms. A woman bearing that name would surly be one of substantial power and influence.

[400] HK of the M. H. T. of S 1927 Chap. 45 The Divine Origin Of The Asiatic Nation V7

[401] E - represents the element of Air reflects the importance of intellectual activities and mental energies in the growth of those who have this primary vowel within their name. Because E associated with Air, it also associated with those chakras of the head-the throat. (creative expression), which reconciles the brow(feminine energy) and the crown (masculine energy).

[402] Thoughts out of the ethereal realm of mind into physical manifestation. The mystical sciences is also known as Reincarnation.

awakening and using the higher mind. The mystical science is the mystical vowels, The vowel sounds in most ancient alphabets were sacred. Vowels have the activating or life-giving power.

> **"The ethers cause these powers to be, and thought of Elohim, of angel, man, or other thinking things, directs the force; when it has done its work the power is no more."** HK of the M. H. T. of S 1927 Chap. 7 Prophet Noble Drew Ali.

The power of the vowel sounds within the human voice can porduce two aspects of sound. One is the vowel sound, which contain the real power which hold the strongest influence upon us. and the other is the is the consonant which could not be discerned without the vowel sounds. Keep in mind that the Prophets teachings are much deeper than you think, for you and I to know we must know thyself.

To know thyself is to open the Divine mysteries and the hidden things of the Soul in order to uncover the truth. If you listen and remember faithfully the melody which reaches you, you will grow and your being will be illumined and you will learn the meaning of the mystery which surrounds you, and that is only in the perfect union of you.

You will find yourself a part of the great harmony from which springs wisdom, the knowledge of the one light which illumines your life and makes all that in the past appeared mysterious open and clear to your eyes. Learn of the earth, the waters, the forests, the flowers, the birds and beast. Nature's countless mirrors reflects the Universal Creator. Therefore look to nature and learn the secrets they hold for you, and the book of Life will be open for you.

One must also study the rules of the seven universal laws and to know its rules which govern human life. (Mental, Correspondence, Vibration, Polarity, Gender, Rhythm and Cause & Effect).Therefore you must desire to understand the laws of nature should first attempt to free yourselves from the laws which seem to hold you.

Some may be thinking of mans law, man has no laws, man only uses rules and regulations and call them laws and when you accept that in your mind you have just created your own individual prison in which you need to fight with countless times, codes and terms to set you free. Think on this, your true deed. Is the deed of the soil wherever you exist. Be the master of the seven and you will comprehend the true meaning of Love, Truth, Peace, freedom and Justice.

The Mystical Science of Know Thyself

"Know thyself and the pride of His creation, the Line[403] uniting divinity[404] and matter; behold a part of Allah Himself within thee"[405]

The outsiders may call it the mystery system, simply because it was a mystery to them. To the infinite mind, it is to Know Thyself and this was the ultimate goal for the pupil. Prophet Noble Drew Ali has given us the divine instructions in his pamphlet[406] of 1927 so that we may obtain from a finite point of view which will develop into a infinite wisdom of the true self. Mind is matter and matter is the doorway to what is known as the fourth dimension or the plane of energy. Energy and matter are different manifestations of mind. There is an energetic field which surrounds the head called the mind field. This atmosphere carry thoughts which produce love or hate given by society or you can call it positive and negative thoughts. This is the reason why Prophet Noble Drew Ali said: **"That we**

---

[403] Line - A matter of course of procedure determined by a specified factor

[404] Divinity - The birthright of inner divinity, which every human being inherit. For this is the wisdom of the Uni-verse, because something is added to thee, unlike to what thou seest; something informs thy clay, higher than all is the object thy senses.

[405] HK of the M. H. T. of S 1927 Chap. 36 Know Thyself V10

[406] Pamphlet - The origins of the word 'pamphlet' are Greek (Egyptian), and it means "loved by all"

need to learn to Love instead of hate" I came across a book by Deepak Chopra[407] **"The Way of The Wizard"** Understanding the lesson:

> "As long as you have fear,[408] you cannot really love. As long as you have anger, you cannot truly love. As long as you have selfish ego, you cannot truly love."

Imagine a intellectual thought from a selfish person possessed with a carnal knowledge who is puffed up in their own conceit and boast of superior under -standing, sends out his/her own invisible hate and poisonous influence to any distance that surrounds that person. The outcome will supply ignorant, selfish, or weak-minded individuals controlling their emotions. This hate is simply an artificial mind set, but it has its cause and effects. Therefore you must learn to love and bare in mind to learn without thought and you are blind; thinking without learning is dangerous. Lesson to learn:

> **"He who learns but does not think is lost! He who thinks but does not learn is in great danger."**

Now, truth is evolved from the within towards the without. Therefore seek to reach the within by the pathway of love through wisdom of the true self. To know thyself you should think about this:

> **"To know what you know and to know what you don't know that is real wisdom."**

Humble is the way towards the soul, this is very important, why?

---

[407] Deepak Chopra born 1947 in New Delhi, India is a physician, a holistic health and alternative medicine practitioner author of 70 books. 1995 "The Way Of The Wizard"

[408] HK of the M. H. T. of S 1927 Chap. 37 The Breath Of Heaven V13 Fear and dismay, who rob thy countenance of its ruddy splendor? Avoid guilt, and thou shalt know that fear is beneath thee, that dismay is unamely.

Because you are to seek the soul through silent meditation[409] guided by love, this is to be attained by centralization of the soul within, with the form without; this gains a very superior state, by means of self-trance. When this condition has been reached, the pupil will have full perception of the subjective world and it's surroundings conditions. And behold the spirit has utterly mastered the flesh. This is also what was meant, when Jesus said:

"In flesh of man there is the essence of the resurrection[410] of the dead[411]. The essence quickened by the Holy Breath will raise the substance of the Body to higher tone."[412]

The resurrection takes place in us every time we rise to Love's realization of the perpetual indwelling life that is connecting us with the Universal Creator and life comes to all who open their minds and like a flood of light, a heaven will come and bring a boundless joy. The great opportunity of the human birth is to transcend the ego[413] mind, through perfect knowledge and devotion, and thereafter remain as the natural mind, The Supreme Being. A well known kept secret is to get Love, you must first give Love. To learn to Love another, you must first Love yourself. Love needs to be uncovered from the layers of fear, jealously and aggression. Real Love is not an emotion it is the truth and the truth cannot pass away, once you have realize this, your resurrection becomes a fact. One of many reasons why

---

[409] HK of the M. H. T. of S 1927 Chap. 12 How to Obtain eternal happiness V1 "In silent mediation Jesus sat beside a flowing spring."

[410] Resurrection - The restoring of the mind and body to their original, undying state.

[411] Dead or Death - This is known as first death of light and life of the Soul in mans consciousness.

[412] HK of the M. H. T. of S 1927 Chap. 17 V35

[413] Ego - The ego of itself is possessed of nothing. It is a mere ignorant child of innocence floating in the Mind of Being. It is the adverse ego that causes all the trouble in the world. It's selfishness and greed in this false expression that looks upon itself as great, honorable, mighty, supreme egoism stops the flow of spiritual life in the organism. " The very mind that you see causing trouble, is the very mind you are becoming: and we don't see. And such is the subtlety of this illusion that we fall into delusion" Mooji.

we cannot comprehend Love, is that we invested so much to become what we are not. Then when its time to return to what we truly are, we afraid to be given up something that we are not. You are not who you be thinking you are or who you conditioned to believe you are. There is something deeper then personality or behind the mind itself which is not our thinking being, because we are aware of our thoughts, there must be something deeper then the mind. Now, if you would mount onto her throne, first bow thyself at her footstool; if you would arrive at the knowledge of her, first inform thyself of your own ignorance. Because real knowledge is to know the extent of one's ignorance and the Essence of knowledge is, having it to use. One who is fully awake is totally at one with this awareness which is independent of thinking mind it is the state of pure being. I have been on this path with the prophet's teachings for 28 years as a faithful member, and I have witnessed and heard just about everything you could have imagine. I have learned that Love must at all times be governed by reason for it to be a positive force, which was the very first principle that Prophet Noble Drew Ali was teaching.

"Act - 3 Love, Truth, Peace, Freedom and Justice must be proclaimed and practiced by all members"

P is the 16th letter (1+6=7) in which the total of 7 the symbol of Spirituality and refers to the divine law of perfection for the divine-natural man. My personal experience is my personal experience, your personal experience is your personal experience. I have only shared a portion of my gift in which it was given to me, to be given to you. This is known as Unity, for it was to build ones awareness of his/her measure of thoughts.[414] For the wise man who truly comprehend thought vibrations of Love which are energies sent out by force and power. The moving force within the idea that gives it expression. There is a law of Spirit that equalize all forces

---

[414] Thought - A product of thinking; a mental vibration or impulse. Each thought is an identity that has central center, around which all elements revolve. Thoughts are capable of expressing themselves. Everythought clothes itself in a life form according to character given it by the thinker. The form is simply the conclusion of the thought.

generated by the mind. This law is in keeping of the divine Principle by using thought energies guided by wisdom.

There is a reason for Prophet Noble Drew Ali's Divine Instructions and for its purpose which is for you to instruct your mind to evolve in your way of thinking and not just to recite his words as if it was a poem, and you don't do anything with them. These Divine Instructions was not given to you for you to know, these Divine Instructions was given to you to Be. So do not worry about the things that you do not know, but be cautious in appraising how you apply what you do know.

GRATITUDE

As the branches of a tree return their sap to the root, from whence it arose;as a river poureth its streams to the sea, whence the spring was supplied; so the heart of a grateful man delighted in returning a benefit received. MHK Chp. 33

Brother (Harry) Hommett A. El was born July 21, 1908 in Pinewood, South Carolina to Harry and Sarah Anderson. Brother Hommett united in the Moorish Holy Temple of Science of the World in 1928. At the age of 20, before the end of 1928 he entered into the Adept Chamber by Prophet Noble Drew Ali. He said: **"When The Prophet looked at him and said come closer, then he whispered something to him in his ear and the Prophet stood back and held his finger up and said don't you never forget that."** With that said it left impact on him for the rest of his life. When the prophet passed away, he was there during the last rights of honor. What he witness was an infinte experience only he can see. He said: **"As the form of the prophet was laid out he raise up and then turned his head at me and winked. He said no one else had witness this and no one believed him.**[415]**"**

He said that the Moors were doing and saying very strange things during the service. Local Chicago paper title "laid to Rest" Followers Mourn Moorish Leader Thus was said:

> **"Lay members of the cult were not to averse to talking about their dead leader, his work and his position on each. Allah's is their god, Islam, their religion and Drew Ali, their prophet. One elderly women whispered to a friend. The "Prophet" was not ill his work was done and he laid his head upon the lap of one of his followers and passed out. In reference to a successor of Drew another remarked, that the prophet's spirit will come back and enter the body of one of the governors.**[416]**"**

Eighteen days after the passing of the prophet, Brother John Givens El, (The Prophet Chauffer) Made the announcement that he was Prophet

---

[415] Infinte experience- the mystical sciences of the conscious mind: There is a divine thought at the root of all esistence. At the touch of its secret spring this divine thought may be brought to light in him. This thought rest in the recesses of every mind and comes forth when least expected. The mind that makes one know one's mental operations and the knowledge or realzation of any idea, object, or condition. This visualization of this experience is of a ascend conciousness that will rise to the spiritual realms of mind known as Waken Vision.

[416] One must take notice that there has been a lot of things that has been said about the Prophet during this time, some were true and faithful followers and some were not. You will need a open mind to those things which were said even if it does not make sense to you. The reason why is that our minds were so much indoctrinated by the oppressor we can't even think for ourselves from a finite and infinite point of view. The Prophets Moorish Movement was in distress, and so he absolutely knew how to succor the situation. Please do not get confused with your emotions of judgment but some may or may not comprehend what he did before he veil his form. The Prophet declared the following, "I have my number, and my work of redeeming you people is finished, and I most go now, or I can't return, and if I don't return, I can't deliver you, and if I don't deliver you, my coming is in vain." He also made a statement "Children, when I make my return, will you know me?" Prophet Noble Drew Ali even paid for his own funeral.

Noble Drew Ali Reincarnated. News was spread throughout the Moorish community. When Brother Hommett heard about this he said he did not believe it until he went to see him he said:

> " I went to see Brother Prophet at 447 East 40th Street, A brother open the door and greeted me with Islam. He said Brother Prophet will be right out to see you, I thought sense I was here I will be needing another fez. Brother Prophet came out and said Islam and then he said: "I will be right back," soon as he came back he had a fez and I thought to myself I did not say anything to him about a new fez. He place the Fez on my head and said lean over here and he whispered the same thing he told me before and stated: "did I not say, don't you never forget that.[417]"

During the World War II period Bro. Hommett was drafted into the U.S Arm forces, then young teacher of Temple No. 6 Richmond, VA. He went through the regular basic training, later shipped West to Oakland, California and assigned to the Army Military Police. While in the army Bro. Hommett visited the Reincarnatated Prophet in Chicago which was very inspiring to him. Others who were in the Arms Services also visted Bro. Prophet. While in the army the young teacher never did give up teaching Isalm. Soon the company which was shilled out to the Pacific Islands, where North America was heavily engaged with Japanese government in the war, (World War II) Soon before time was up, Bro. Hommett using the Holy Koran, came out of the army and with an honorable discharge. His intentions now was to live in California and open a Temple. He had already gathered a small group of Asiatics followers. Back in Chicago, Bro. Prophet had different plans for the Brother. He sent a telegram or a letter saying that he wanted to see the young teacher. Bro. Hommett didn't leave right away. He still thought he was going to have a Temple in California.

---

[417] Every time Brother Hommett shared his experience about meeting the Reincarnated Prophet, There was this elated expression on his face and at that moment it seemed as though time had stood still. It was a very spiritual event for him.

As related by Bro. Hommett; Bro. Prophet came to him in spirit.[418] Bro. Hommett still would not go, so he was laid flat on his back in bed until he made up his mind to visit the Reincarnated Prophet. When Bro. Hommett made up his mind to go to Chicago, he was able to move. He went to Chicago and Bro. Prophet told of his experience. Bro. Hommett then went back to Temple No. 6, and started teaching again. As a teacher he spoke of many experiences he witness seeing the founder, Prophet Noble Drew Ali. He told many times how the founder always kept a stern serious look on his face. Bro. Hommett was well known around the circle for admitting his wrongness, no matter what came up. He said on one occasion, "Yes, the Father whip me, good." During those days the teachers were trying to keep the young teacher off balance. One meeting a teacher would speak on nationality, the other from the religious side, the other from the Prophet's words and so forth, covering about every subject they could think of. With all the talking the audience would almost come to their feets with "Praise Allah!, go on, speak it." After they all had spoken they finally gave the Holy Koran to Bro. Hommett, knowing they had the young teacher beat.[419] Bro. Hommett A. El gets up, takes the Holy Koran, looks at the teachers who were seated with him behind the rostume. Each one having a smile on their faces. Bro. Hommett Looks towards the wall, also Behind him. He looks at the pictures of Prophet Noble Drew Ali and Prophet Noble Drew Ali Reincarnated, the Divine Constitution and the Charter. He started speaking from the Charter, why it was made, what purpose it seved the movment and etc. Bro. Hommett El spoke with such forcefulness, that the audience responded with "Praise Allah and speak on." The teachers looked at each other and shook their heads, laughing. They couldn't catch the young teacher off balance.[420] There were other Teachers, Asst. Teachers

---

[418] Brother Prophet told him in the spirit, that he would not move until he made up his mind to visit him. Now, Brother Prophet spent more time with Bro. Hommett then any anyone around the Moorish circle.

[419] This was all done in fun among the teachers.

[420] From well informed Moorish sources, (the teacher) it was said pulled the same trick on the young teacher For years, but Bro. Hommett always ended on top. He was schooled to be a disciple of Prophet Noble Drew Ali/ Prophet Noble Drew Ali Reincarnated for

and outstanding Moorish Americans who all can not be witten about, but will also be remembered for what they also did for the Moorish National and Divine Movement. (This information was excerpts taken from The Biography of The Moors Part II and III by Bro. Claudas M. El).

THE MYSTICAL SCIENCE OF REINCARNATION

There has been many concepts of reincarnation by world religions. Some today still leaves a mystery in its explanation. Some religions stop teaching it because it did not fit in with their doctrine. Whatever, the case may be. What we do know is that man don't die[421] and that reincarnation[422] is to return in another form after the physical death of the body, then we will return all over again with the process of being born again. However there is another science of reincarnation that has been researched for years, it is known as telepathy transmission.[423] It is known that the Egyptians believed in reincarnation or transmigration of the soul. This was one of the mystical science[424] that Prophet Noble Drew Ali knew. Reincarnation is when a soul

---

the future generation to come. In later years in Newark N.J. M. S. T of A No. 10 at a time of unrest conditions Bro. Hommett stay silence for 3 years. And it was at that time that he received a spiritrual awakening From Allah to restore The Moorish Holy Temple of Science.This was put back in place in the year of 1980. By 1981 Bro. James A. El from Tempe N0.6 Richmond VA. also had a vision from a dream to follow the path. Bro. Hommett ordained Bro. James and he became the assistance Grand Shiek of the M. H. T. of S. Upon the passing of Bro. Hommett in 1994 at the age of 86 Bro. James became the Grank Sheik, in 2004 Bro James pass at the age of 79.

[421] HK of the M. H. T. of S 1927 Ch. I The Creation And Fall Of Man "Man cannot die; the spirit-man is one with Allah, and while Allah lives man cannot die.

[422] Reincarnation - re means "back, again" incarnation meaning "a new embodiment" another name for reincarnation in the year of 1812 was rebirth. re "renewed life" birth "activity" 1833.

[423] Telepathy Transmission (6th and 7th sense) Extrasensory psychic communication directly from one person's mind to the fifth dimension (A state of Heaven…the plane of light which is the highest realms a soul can reach). The Planet Saturn has the influence to interact in Telepathy. This was done on Aug. the 7th 1929. Note: recorded in a book Aspect of the Heavens For July and Aug. 1929. States: " For the summer months of July and Aug. the only planet favorably situated for observation during the evening hours is Saturn."

[424] Mystical Science (Spiritual Science) is the systematic and orderly arrangement of

leaves the body, it rest for a season. Then innate desire for material expression asserts itself, and it seeks the primal mind. Reincarnation is the result of man's use of the great forces of Mind, enabling a soul that has been separated from the vehicle of ex- pression (the body) again to attract to it the necessary substance to reconstruct the body-consciousness and have another opportunity for the demonstration of the Truth of Being. The law of reincarnation is the law of cause and effect which governs the progress of Man's evolution[425] whilst incarnate upon the Earth. Nothing is ever lost, but both spirit and matter are subject to change according to the planes of thought upon which they function. Now lets seek into the reincarnation of Prophet Noble Drew Ali from a spiritual view point. Brother John Givens El[426] united in the Temple in 1925 the same year that the founder announce his prophet-hood he was also the chauffeur[427] and mechanic[428] for Prophet. He went through the adept chamber the same year, to share some light you may never know what the Prophet was teaching him during those private moments as brother John was driving him around. Later in years The Prophet took ill,[429] he knew that his health was not getting any better and so he made a statement only to a few Moors. The Prophet said:

---

knowledge. Spiritual Science, which is the orderly arrangement of the truths of Being, does not always conform to intellectual standards, but it is still scientific. Spiritual Science treats of absolute ideas, while mental science treats of limited thoughts. Idea which means a mental pattern of perfection.

[425] Evolution -The development achieved by man working under spiritual law. It is a result of the development of ideas in mind. What we are is the result of the evolution of our consciousness, and this consciousness is the result of seed ideas sown in the mind. Evolution is the unfolding in consciousness of that which the Universal Creator involved in man in the beginning.

[426] Brother John Givens El 1904 - 1945 John means "Allah's gracious gift."

[427] Chauffeur - the science is that a chauffeur drives another form wherever he needs to go. With that being said; Brother John was to use his form to carry on what the founder has intended, through his works, words and deeds.

[428] Mechanic - One who repairs (he was to spiritually repair the damages that was done by the early Moors).

[429] A statement made by the Defender Newspaper - Drew Ali laid to rest- Hundreds of Chicagoans attended the funeral last week of Noble Drew Ali, founder of the Moorish Temple, who died at his home after a long illness.

"When I make my return, I will be wearing a size 17 collar and a number 9 shoe.[430]"

At that time, Prophet Noble Drew Ali was wearing a size 15 collar and a number 8 shoe. Now 17 / 1+7= 8 which mean infinity and as you will see both 8+8 = 16 / 6+1=7 now remember what the Prophet said? "I have my number" The Prophet's number was seven. The number 9 represent serving humanity and 15 is 1+5= 6 and Brother John was born on the 6th day. The Prophet suddenly past form July 20, 1929 at 9:50 pm on a Friday at the age of 43.[431] The date of his burial was July 26, 1929 on a Friday, The body was placed at lot 44 and site 7. 18 days later on August 7, 1929 Brother John Givens El finds his spiritual dawn, now an atmosphere of newly organized spiritual force, glancing back at the past he catches glimpses of development from Prophet Noble Drew Ali. The spiritual conscious that he inherited through the long reign of 18 days. The Soul of man[432] being between spirits of such wide differences, those who always contemplate the divine essence of the Soul Spirit can raise itself to one or sink itself to the other. Let it be known that according to the goal which each Soul has reached on earth during its life pilgrimage will be its first starting point in Spirit life. And as his un ripened Soul must pass its way only through long ages of self elaborating effort, until it reaches the arche-type, thence passing on into its angel -hood, becoming a perfected Soul.

Thus a living guide; a beacon light[433] of hope for the Moorish Nation, for progressing ever onward and upward, a messenger of Love. Brother

---

[430] Symbolic meaning of the Shoe - Represent the words with which understanding (Truth) is clothed.

[431] July 20, 1929 the previous year on the same date on the back of our Questionnaire July 20, 1928 was the date of our Religious Corporation some thing to really think about. It was on a Friday when he departed out of flesh again something to think about. He was 43 / 4+3= 7 his number. (July is the 7th month).

[432] HK of the M. H. T. of S 1927 Chap. 38 "The Soul Of Man" V23 Her motion is perpetual; her attempts are universal. Is it beyond the regions of the stars? Yet will her eye discover it. Inquiry is her delight. The soul that thirsteth after knowledge.

[433] Ibid. Chap. I "The Creation And The Fall Of Man" "Thus hope will ever be his beacon light: there is no failure for the human soul, for Allah is leading on and victory is sure."

John was reaching out nearer and nearer toward Noble Drew Ali's Spiritual essences and at last entering his divine principals, resting finally in the bosom of the absolute Love, in which came the guidance and guardianship of our beloved Prophet. And now awaking to a knowledge that he has a Soul Spirit and that of Prophet Noble Drew Ali are merging thoughts recognizing that there is an inner man and life as well as the objective life of the outer man, and that he is made more strong, more noble, with a greater force[434] of potentiality and attributes of Prophet Noble Drew Ali, by the inner life of Truth and Spirit than he ever conceived possible. He now finds that his better part of being has been made more Spiritual conscious by the perfect serenity of this high and sacred dual Love diffuses over his heart of mind.[435] Brother John is now lifted to such a height of Love with this con -nection of the Prophet spiritual information. He finds about him, now an atmosphere of newly organized Spiritual force of reincarnation. Here is a very interesting insight that I have discovered. The symbols of 7, 8, 6 and 9 are the revealing signs of the one who was helping the Moorish movement to march forward toward the nobler life which the future holds for the races of men.

Noble Drew Ali - DOB Jan 8, 1886 PAST July 20, 1929
$$1 + 8 = 9 \qquad 7 + 2 = 9$$

$9 + 9 = 18$ days of The Reincarnation / 8th month Aug 7, 1929
$$8 + 7 = 15/6$$

John Givens El - DOB Dec 6, 1904 - PAST Oct 21, 1945
$$6$$
The sign $= 6$
The path$=9$ 69 which is the secret science of numerology for **Reicarnation**

---

[434] Ibid. Chap. 7 V16 "Force is the will of Allah and is omnipotent."

[435] The Mystical Science of the mind is that there is a power in a thought and it is your 6th sense (intuition) which for Wisdom speaks from out the highest plane of spirit life. Thoughts are invisible current as air. Here is an example: have you ever experience, that someone was talking to you and they said something exactly what you were thinking about. Well, that is known as intuition, so imagine if someone taught you how to master it into its highest level.

One must know by knowing the meaning of numbers and letters, we can interpret the relation of words to each other. With this knowledge you will unveil its hidden meaning.

The **69** is identical to the astrological sign Cancer ♋ :July 20 was 2 days before a new sign begins, this was important because it was the time of year when nature renews[436] itself. When you add 6 and 9 we will get 15 the prophet's collar size 15/6:6 represent the body, 1 is the individual life force in the body, 5 is the five senses. There are 13 letters in reincarnation. The number of letters tells the traits of the word. 13 is the scared number of the inhabitants of Afru-ika, and the 13 refers to the 13th letter, which is M and the ancients' symbol for water was M. It is in the waters of the womb that the fetus takes form and becomes the baby that is to be a living soul. M is life and death, renewal and regeneration. It is the end of the old and transformation into the new. (And this the trait of reincarnation) **Prophet Noble Drew Ali Reincarnated** was the transformation of the Spiritual Soul infomation from the founder.

∙∙

---

[436] Renew is a rebirth of the soul inductive bodies which is defined as the mystical science of reincarnation.Throughtout all the regions of limitess space, Spirit and Spiritual energy, when viewed from the highest altitude attainable by human conception, become merged into the great Absolute and Universal Spirit.

The Moors of 1943 honoring Prophet Noble Drew Ali and Prophet Noble Drew Ali Reincarnated.

The Great meeting is still on! Prophet Noble Drew Ali Reincarnated encourage the Moors to continue with all businesses and even the Moorish schools etc. He was teaching the Moors their culture and customs and the Divine Sciences within the Moorish Holy Koran, but only to the faithful few. When he took his first photo it was 19(34) 3+4=7 the

Prophets number. One photo is with a cape on and the other without the cape.[437] When he made his announcement that he was back in Sept which was the 9th month, at the second Moorish convention. The unbelievers did not accept him, but he tarried not, among the Moors was one, a generous soul who had faith in the reincarnated Prophet and then the Prophet went with him and in his home abode. His home was at 447 East 40 Street. Yes! The same number as the grave site of the founder. (lot 44 site 7) The signs do tell and express the truth. *The science of the scared vowel 0 in John is the element of water and Cancer as well. This reflects lessons in learning to breathe new life into old circumstances. Cancer is the mother of the Astrological sign and the moon is her planetary symbol.

Life Lesson of Resurrection

Truth is but one; thy doubts are of thine own raising. He who made virtues what they are, planted in thee a knowledge of their pre-eminence. Act as thy soul dictates to thee, and the end shall be always right.

---

[437] This demonstration was unveiling the form. Remember this that every object in a picture tells a story.

Teach him science, and his life shall be useful.

Resurrection, reincarnation and incarnation, are levels of the Soul, which are develop from leaning that the subconscious mind is the vehicle through which the spirit works when receiving thoughts and inspiration from outside the physical body. When you think a thought with a loving conscious brain you will set in motion a thought potential which will radiate, like the ripples on a pond, that represent vibrations sending out into a universal atmosphere. When you meditate the brain, you are allowing the portals of the spiritual bridge or subconscious mind to open, then your inspiration, or a creative thought-force, flow in from the layers of spirit to which you are attuned, and by crossing the subconscious bridge, you will pass into the relaxed conscious brain, thus materializing those things which have been received, so that the thought from spirit will become the written or spoken word to give knowledge to the material plane.

Remember, when a spirit of a prophet, sage, hierophant and wise men has passed out of their mortal body that obtains the key to all knowledge. That information is forthwith available in its dimensions, you can only receive this if you have mastered Love, Truth, Peace, Freedom and Justice. Which are advanced energy levels that you must learn in time.

The Adept chamber represent the earth school from which man is progressively learning of his origin and reason for being. Through these lessons in the fullness of time you will be brought to realize that true knowledge comes only to those who can absorb spirit and matter in one indivisible whole. The spirit then will rise to higher levels of cosmic knowledge.

The spirit is a magnetic potential which exist within your human bodies. The body is only an vehicle to enclose that spirit. Only by experience can the lessons which lead to final at-one-ment be mastered. The Soul of Man is the same in essence as the original creative universal force. By opening up the temple of the Soul, the spirit of Man is endowed with the power of the creative universal force. Learn those mysteries which belong only to those who seek them through self-discipline and overcoming of those lower emotions which are born of the flesh.

The thoughts of Allah, are the everlasting of the past unto the never ending days to come. And so is man, the spirit-man.

My final Thoughts

When you enter the **Prophets Temple** at various meetings, leave all your earth cares and troubles outside. Discuss not its various ills or wants, but try and bring the mind in rapport with the spiritual thoughts and ideas. The mind should be in a passive state rather than an active state, pure thoughts by Love of Truth and of humanity. One should not desire anything in particular, but unite in being pleased to receive that which is best for all. A meeting may produce most important results, not only for those who take part in it, but also for those of who may not know. But in order that it may do this, the member must comprehend the hidden side of the meeting, and must work with a view to produce the highest possible effects. Many members utterly overlook this most important part of their work, and have in consequence quite an unworthy idea of what of a Temple is. There are at times that a member may feel that some meetings are often rather dull, and so they do not always attend them. A member who may feel this has not grasped the most spiritual truth about the work of a Temple: He/She may find its meetings are not interesting to them and they think that they are better off at home.

The person who attends a meeting for the sake of what he/she can get, or to be entertained there, is thinking of themselves only and not of his Temple or of the Moorish Society. We should join the **Moorish Temple** not for anything that we get from it, but because, having satisfied ourselves of the truth of what it proclaims. We join it for the sake of spreading the teaching, and for the sake of understanding it better by discussing it with those whom have spent years in trying to live it. We who belong to it and get a good deal from it, in the way of the Prophets Divine instructions and of help in understanding difficult points, of brotherly feeling and of kindly thoughts. The whole life of a member ought to be devoted to trying to fill his or hers place well, and to do their duty to the utmost of their power. Every member should have an intelligent comprehension of a subject, which is to be considered, and should be prepared to contribute their share of information with regard to it.

In this way every member has their work to do, and each is greatly helped to a full and clear comprehension of the matter under consideration because all present are thus earnestly fixing their thought upon it. Each must go to the meeting in Spirit of helpfulness, thinking of what he or she can contribute and in what way he or she can be useful, for upon the attitude of mind much depends on one's ability to learn from within his or hers Spirit. (This is Wisdom) A member/student must compre- hend the difference between thinking and knowing. Thinking involves the manipulation of symbols and knowing what occurs in there absence. To Know, you must shut down the thinking process. " Let us forget the flesh and go with mind into the land of fleshless things: mind never does forget. And backward through the age's master minds can trace themselves; and thus they know.

Many noble-hearted souls have been calling for unity. This trend has gained in momentum over the last few decades. Yet, despite the popular growth in movements for unity, we still find conflict and discord in the nation. Speeches and conferences are motivated by high ideas. They inspire the participants to turn their attention to the goal of oneness. But unity comes about only at the personal level, when each one experiences it for one 's self. When we merge in **Allah** and see the Light of **Allah** in every being, we have truly realized unity. It becomes easy for us to Love all, because we see our own self in each being. If we truly wish to achieve human equality, we must experience it ourselves. Just imagine what a beautiful nation we would have if every Moor saw **Allah's** Light in every other being. There would be an atmosphere of peace and tranquility in all. Our spiritual leaders will speak to us lovingly, they embrace us affectionately, and they carte for us from the depths of their heart just like the Prophet.

This is the result of being in the company of someone who has merged with **Allah** and our Prophets teachings. What they have attained is possible for each of us to attain. Wouldn't it be wonderful if we felt this love and harmony radiating from everyone in the **Prophets Temple. The Temple** was meant to be a garden of Eden and a heaven of bliss. To attain such a paradise in…our Temple, each of us to make a contribution. Peace and unity begin within each one of us. We cannot expect others to radiate harmony and oneness if we ourselves are not prepared to see their fruition in our own lives. Each of us must do their own small part to bring about the fulfillment of this Noble Life.

We can attain this condition by the process of mediation that leads to self-knowledge and **Allah's** realization. When we begin to have love for all, a transformation occurs within us. Our whole behavior towards others changes. we become nonviolent in all our dealings. We begin to have understanding and compassion towards the idiosyncrasies and habits of others. We stop criticizing people in our minds. First, we realize that they are bound by the shrouds of ignorance and illusion of this world. We know that deep within them is the soul, apart of **Allah**, and that it is only their mind and their state of spiritual ignorance that causes them to behave the way they do. Second, we are so steeped in Allah's love and bliss which permeates us that we do not want to be distracted from that rapturous state by petty thoughts of others.

We are so far removed from the trifles that people become involved in that we do not recognize them.. Criticizing others in our thoughts only pulls us away from the state of happiness that union with Allah brings. Since our thoughts will be filled with divine love of **Allah**, our words will become sweet and loving. We will not say anything unkind to anyone. People who come within our sphere will find words of love and kindness. They will not do to other men what they would not have other men do unto them, because they see **Allah's** Light within all creation. When this unity is attained, the divisions that separate human beings from one anther will fall away. Remember that segregation lead to weakness and lack of cohesion, which in turn leads to vulnerability when the links of the chain are made of different material, the chain can be more easily broken. Do not allow the chain to be broken!

No one has the right to dictate the road to immorality or sit in judgment on a fellow-being, and none has a right to think a thing is true simply because they want it to be so. They who claims to have the whole truth in any direction closes the door to reception of more light and truth in that direction. **Prophet Noble Drew Ali** teachings is the key to everything in our life; men/women stands out alone as a goal; every- thing in life builds up to them, then beyond; not externally, but having reached man/woman, the development goes on within. He or she must be developed out of life. We need the Prophet's religion of Love, Truth, Peace, Freedom and Justice, that will make it a duty to see that our future men and women be taught to believing in the capacity to succeed in life.

The teaching's of the Prophet must of necessity be one of perfect charity, pure love, an unfaltering faith, with a divinely trusting hope and belief that can be demonstrated beyond a doubt. Based upon such a safe foundation, with the assured aid so all the good of past and present time. Shall not such a union of spiritual strength work wonders? Indeed! A charity that gives to reach a perfect right to individual belief, ready and willing to take those who differ by the hand in all harmony, and listen to their mode of thought in brotherly love. A love so pure that, an injury to one is the concern to all; that each shall help bear the others' burden, thus lightening sorrows and sharing together all joys; every heart shall be ready to respond to those in need, poverty, sickness or to rejoice with the happy and prosperous. A faith made sure by more than promises; by actual words that is able to be fully demonstrated by science and philosophy as well as fact.

A blessed hope, that desires good to all humanity, and divine aspiration of beholding a heaven upon earth, which would certainly be possible if all humanity earnestly endeavored to be unselfish, honest, pure, intelligent, just and industrious believing in the fatherhood of Allah and brotherhood of man. We need the Prophets teachings in which the grand conception of the faith of Mohammed be establish here in American and abroad. Where every man and women is free to develop and grow His/hers spiritual life and utter their best thoughts. We the Moors who live by the teachings in one way, and one another; but the vital and only thing is to love one another and seek to do good to all. The real measure of our beloved Prophet should be the measure of our loving kindness toward one another. Where he said:

" A follower of Islam in the true sense of the word is one whose hands, tongue and thoughts do not hurt others."

By practicing this form and substance we will become one. The manner of expressing it is wholly secondary to what is to be expressed, because we are to first proclaim and practiced Love, Truth, Peace, Freedom and Justice. One of the great question of the day is, can the Moors of the teachings of **Noble Drew Ali** set his Temple's up without practicing malicious feelings and ancient hatred from the past? Can we afford to be without Allah and his Prophet? The temple was not built on the surface of the sand, it was a sure foundation and that foundation is in Noble Drew Ali's doctrines in which contains our hope, aims, rules and articles of religion. Noble Drew Ali's vision was to lift our sights to a higher Spiritual level, and in so doing to enlarge, exalt and inspire. Remember we can be the revealers of the light, but we must have the light before we can reveal the light.

"In these modern days there came a forerunner, who was divinely preared by Allah, and his name is Marcus Garvey, who did teach and warn the nations of the earth to prepare to meet the coming Prophet."

Marcus said:

> "**Nationalism** is necessary. It is political power and control. No race is free until it has a strong nation of its own-its own system of government and its own order of society. It is the only protection of your generation and your race. Hold on to the idea, of an independent government and nation so long as other men have them. The sovereign of a people is in the Nation. It is the people, forming a society of their own to govern themselves and achieve their ends. The flag of a Nation is the emblem that signifies the existence of that Nation. Make your Nation the highest expression of human idealism."

Nationhood is the only means by which modern civilization can completely protect itself. Independence of nationality, independence of government, is the means of protecting not only the individual, but the group. Nationhood is the highest ideal of all peoples. We are moving from one state of organization to another, and we shall so continue until we have thoroughly lifted ourselves into the organization of government. Show me a well organized nation, and I will show you a people and a Nation respected by the world.

Prophet Noble Drew Ali statement of 1928 Moorish Convention:

"The garment I have on represent power and if you obey my voice you will have power with me. I am going to free you though it's hard because of your mixture which brings about many different spirits. When you fail to hear my voice you are lost"

"You! Who are heads of Temples, it is easy for you to destroy the influence of the Temple and me. Now lace up your shoes and get right!"

"You stop figuring out your way how your salvation shall come, just follow me."

"I have done more than you think."

"I am not asleep, it will take you Moors a long time to find out what I did today."

DEDICATION

TO all the true a Divine Prophets and Sages of the Ages. To my Mungin, Williams, Hudson, Dixon and Chisholm family. To my ancestors, spiritual historians and conscious teachers. To my teachers Grand Sheik Brother Hommet A. El and Grand Sheik Brother James A. El. My spiritual guiders Cherubim and Seraphim. To my extended Moorish family and my very close friends. Let Love be the fragrance of your aura, so that one will absorb the pure essence of you. Specal thanks to Sis. Evelyn K El and Bro. Hakim M Bey

THIS BOOK

THIS book was compiled from many different sources, some were historical, philosophical, metaphysical and spiritual expression of events through the signs and symbols of numerology and scared names. At some level it was important for me to give to you some information that may be unfamiliar to your knowledge. Simply because this book was a need to know basis and it requires a very open mind to its contents. You may find some stories and events out of your perimeter, however one must adjust their way of thinking in order to get a glimpse into it's revelations. We have all had spiritual experiences. We have not always had the words for these experiences, so we may not have recognized them for what they were. Therefore we may use different terms for what holds life's mysteries and its deepest meanings for each of us. The most profound spiritual experiences might come to use any time, anywhere.

    Dear Reader, the call is sounded from the Temple Within, saluting you and bidding you to seek on, never wery of well doing; advocating the right of all men to think, to listen, to observe, and to confirm each for yourself upon all questions. Not in the knowledge of things, but in the perfection of the Soul within. Which lies the Empire of man. The powers of the mind are gifts of His goodness. The Kingdom of Allah is not a thought, but an experience. One must try to awaken their internal light. And when that light is lit, amazedly you will find yourself knowing without study what no book could teach you. For you are learning from Spiritual intuition what life is and Allah is. Yes, indeed it is possible for you to learn things without the ordinary auxiliaries. But you must cultivate your Love in order to produce will-power for you to master it. I truly hope that you will gain something from this, for it is my gift to you.

REFERENCES

References

Holy Koran of The Moorish Holy Temple of Science 1927 - Holy Temple which means to the redeemed Mental body. Science is the systematic and orderly arrangement of knowledge, which is the orderly arrangement of truths of Being, does not always conform to intellectual standards, but it is still scientific. This Spiritual science treats of absolute ideas, while mental science treats of limited thoughts. Holy which is whole (complete) - Holistic relating to a whole: including or involving all of something, especially all of somebody's physical, mental, and social conditions, not just physical symptoms, in the treatment of illness

Holy Quran by Maulana Muhamad Ali 7th edition
Power in yor name 1998
Numerology
Moorish literature 1927
Holy Bible King James version
Chicago Daily Tribune 1925
Mis-education of the Nergo 1933
Statements and Prophesies of Noble Drew Ali
Moorish Koran Questionary 1928
M. H. T of S Divine Constitution and By-Laws
Cosmic Consciousness 1913
Aquarian Gospel of Jesus The Christ 1907
Ancient and Modern Britons Vol. I 1884
Goden Age of The Moors 1992
The unknown life of Christ 1894
The Childern of Mu 1931

Footnote 70 - History of the Akasha Records. Akasha is Sanskrit word meaning ether which means in ancient cosmology, the element that filled all space beyond the sphere of the moon, constituting the substance of the stars and planets. Conceived of as a purer form of fire or air, as a fifth element (forces in the universe) This was known as the concept of an etheric library, which are a collection of mystical knowledge that is encoded in the ether on a non-physical plane of existence. Those who champion the truth of the Akasha Records assert that they were accessed by ancient people of various cultures, including the Indian, Moors, Tibetans and other peoples of the Himalaya, Egyptians, Persians and Chinese.

Hard Truth Wake Up America - Google
Metaphysical Dictionary by Charles Fillmore
Satti Majid a Sudanese Missionary to the United States late 1920's
The U.S. A Constitution 13th Amendment 13-20 / 20 sections was with drawn.
World's Great Men of Color 1946
The Montauk Book of The Dead 2005 by Peter Moon
Unto Thee I Grant 1925

References

Footnote 106 - The Six Black Presidents Black Blood: White Mask U.S.A 1993 by

Dr. Auset BaKhufu page 219

Footnote 110 - A Pepole's History of Florida 1513-1876 2009 by Adam Wasserman

The Story of The Moors In Spain 1886

Shamanistic System of The Cherokees - The symbolic color system was as follows:

East = red = success; triumph
North = blue = defeat; trouble
West = black = death
South = white = peace; happiness

Virginia Fugitive Law 1642
Nature Know No Color Line 1952
Gods Gift To America 1961
Sex and Race VI -VII -VIII 1967
Secret Societies A history 1961 by Arkon Daraul Chapter 10 page 111
The Garduna
Holy Warriors of Spain
Afrikan People and European Holidays A Mental Genocide 1979
David Miller On Nationality 1995 National Identity
1791 Virginia Legislative
Africa Presence in Early America 1992
Ancient Egyptian and Chinese in America 1974 by Rafique Ali Jairazbhoy
Saga of America 1980
Phoenix Gazette April 5, 1909
Othello's Children in The New World "Moorish History & Identity in The African American Experience" 2002
BBC News Report November 22,2006
Black Labor White Wealth 1994
The "Negro" Its Origin And Evil Use 1960
Noah Webster Dictionary 1913 - Nationality
100 Amazing Facts About The Negro 1934
The African Origin of Civilization 1955
Black Indians A Hidden Heritage 1986
1790 Moors Sundry Act South Carolina Sumter County
Savannah Georgia Gazette May 24, 1775
Black Laws of Virginia Guild 1936
Muslims in America 1998
The Nanticoke Indians: Past and present 1983
Delaware's Forgotten Folks: The Story of The Moors and Nanticoke 1934

Stolen Legacy 1954

References

Noah Webster Dictionary 1828 - America

Footnote 187 - The Doctrine of Discovery: Papal Bulls of the 15th Century gave Christian explorers the right to claim lands they "discovered" and lay claim to those lands for their Christian Monarchs. Any land that was not inhabited by Christians was available to be "discovered", claimed, and exploited. If the "pagan" inhabitants could be converted, they might be spared. If not, they could be enslaved or killed.

Footnote 196 Frederick Douglass speech " The Meaning of July Fourth For The Negro" July 5, 1852 (Quotes) " This Fourth July is yours, not mine. You rejoice, I must mourn. To drag a man fetters into the grand illuminated temple of liberty, and call upon him to join you in joyous anthems, were inhuman mockery and sacrilegious irony. Do you mean, citizens, to mock me, by asking me to speak today? If so, there is a parallel to your conduct. And let me warn you that it is dangerous to copy the example of a nation whose crimes, towering up to heaven, were thrown down by the breath of the Almighty, burying that nation in irrecoverable ruin! I can today take up the plaintive lament of a peeled and woe-smitten people!" "I do not hesitate to declare, with all my soul, that the character and conduct of this nation never looked blacker to me than on this 4th of July!"

"What, to the American slave, is your 4th of July? I answer; a day that reveals to him, more than all other days in the year, the gross injustice and cruelty to which he is constant victim. To him, your celebration is a sham; your boasted liberty, an unholy license; your national greatness, swelling vanity; your sound of rejoicing are empty and heartless; your denunciation of tyrants brass fronted impudence; your shout of liberty and equality, hollow mockery; your prayers and hymns, your sermons and thanks-givings, with your religious parade and solemnity, are to him, mere bombast, fraud, deception, impiety, and hypocrisy-a thin veil to cover up crimes which would disgrace a nation of savages."

The Sung Document 1178
African Early Presence in Asia 1985
Unexpected Faces in Ancient America 1975
When Rocks Cry Out 2009

OED Oxford English Dictionary 1895- Published by the Oxford University Press,
Oxford University first teachers were Moorish and Jewish scholars from Moorish Andalus (read Golden Age of The Moor page 182 Moorish Spain: Academic Source and Foundation For The Rise And Success of Western European Universities in The Middle Ages by Joes V. Pimienta-Bey). Later in years Europeans such as the London philological Society, which was established in 1842. (unconnected to Oxford University) They formed a " un- registered Words Committee" to search for unlisted and unefined words lacking in current dictionaries. However if you will read from the above book Goden Age of The Moor you will read on page 225: "When one notes the period in which most of Europe's oldest and finest universities were established, one cannot but be struck by the proximity in time the scientific flowering of Moorish Andalus and the establishment of European centers for translation of Moorish documents. (listed below is just a few of European Countries that learned from the Moors)

1158 Bologna (It) - 1180 Montpellier (Fr.) - 1200 Oxford (Eng) - 1245 Rome (It) - 1257 Cambridge (Eng)
The revelation of the above clearly support the contention that Europe's academic ascension was primarily born of its contacts with the Moors who were occupying European soil.

References

Dred Scott v. Sanford (1857) Supreme Court Case
The Way of The Wizard 1995

Metaphysical Dictionary the revealing word by Charles Fillmore (August 22,1854 - July 5, 1948) Founded Unity The New Thought movement in 1889. (New Thought movement are Religious Science, Unity Church and the Church of Divine Science) He became known as an American mystic for his contributions to spiritualist interpretations of biblical Scripture. He studided Shakespeare, Tennyson, Emerson, and Lowell as works on spiritualism, Eastern religions, and metaphysics.

Chicago Defender News paper founded in 1905
The Teachings of Osiris 1927 copied from our Ancient lessons from Khemet.

Brother Claudas W. EL - 1939-1983
Born the eldest son of four children to Brother & Sister William and Dorothy Watson on March 7, 1939 in Newark NJ. One of the most distinguish qualities was his sincere dedication towards the Moorish Divine and National Movement. Having been admitted into the Adept Chamber in the year of 1959, Bro. Claudas soon became a Master Adept and Professor of the Moorish tradition and teacher of the Islamic principles of Love, Truth, Peace, Freedom and Justice. After serving in the capacity of Secretary of Temple No. 10 in Newark. Bro. Claudas moved to Chicago in 1967. A humble servant of Allah and faithful member, he came under the inspirational teachings of many Moors who were taught by the Reincarnated Prophet, Noble Drew Ali. Bro. Claudas became the Grand Sheik of Temple No. 1(Chicago., M.S.T. of A) He was the sixth Sheik to have held this esteem office and authoritative position since the appointment of Brother Compton Johnson El by the Reincarnated Prophet to post in 1929. It was Brother Claudas Wastson El who wrote the first Biography of the Moors.

Words from Prophet Noble Drew Ali Reincarnated: " You all must remember that ALLAH is all. When people learn better they act better. Just the way you see people acting that is the way they are thinking."

The Hierarchy of Angels
Ice Man Inheritance 1978
The Declaration of Independence formally declared on July 2, 1776
The Holy Science 1894
Essential Sufism 1997
The Doctrine of The Sufis 1966
A Chronology of The Bible 1973
The Upanishads 1907

www.ingramcontent.com/pod-product-compliance
Lightning Source LLC
Chambersburg PA
CBHW070623300426
44113CB00010B/1631